RED

ACKNOWLEDGEMENTS

John Agard: "Sonnet 13" from *Clever Backbone* (Bloodaxe Books, 2009); Patience Agbabi: "Seeing Red", "Foreign Exchange", "Comedown" and "Sol", from *Bloodshot Monochrome* (Canongate Books, 2008); Moniza Alvi: "The Sleeping Wound" from *Europa* (Bloodaxe Books, 2008); Faustin Charles: "The Red Robber" from *Children of the Morning: Selected Poems* (Peepal Tree Press, 2008); Fred D'Aguiar: "The Never-Never" from *Continental Shelf* (Carcanet, 2009); Imtiaz Dharker: "How to Cut a Pomegranate" from *The Terrorist at my Table* (Bloodaxe Books, 2006); Tishani Doshi: "Homecoming" and "Sunrise at Sanchi Stupa" from *Countries of the Body* (AARK ARTS, 2006), "Ode to the Walking Woman", commissioned by the Tate for *Tate Etc.*, (Issue 9, 2007); Crista Ermiya: "Three Days Red" and "Agnes" from *Piranha* (iD on Tyne, 2007); Khadijah Ibrahiim: "When My Time Come" from *Rootz Runnin'* (Inscribe/Peepal Tree Press, 2008); Linton Kwesi Johnson: "Five Nights of Bleeding" from *Mi Revalueshanary Fren: Selected Poems*, (Penguin, 2002); Anthony Joseph: "Bougainvillea: Super 8 Red" from *Bird Head Son* (Salt Publishing, 2009); Jackie Kay: "The Red Graveyard" and "Pride" from *Darling: New & Selected Poems* (Bloodaxe Books, 2007), and "Bush Fire" and "Red Running Shoes" from *Red, Cherry Red* (Bloomsbury, 2007); Judith Lal: "Red, As Red As You Like" from *Flageolets at the Bazaar* (Smith/Doorstop Books, 2007); Segun Lee-French: "Breathing Palm Oil" from *Praise Songs For Aliens* (Suitcase Books, 2009); Jack Mapanje: "Retinal Screening, Christmas 2006" from *Beasts of Nalunga* (Bloodaxe, 2007); Karen McCarthy: "Routemaster" and "Pomegranate Slicers" from *The Worshipful Company of Pomegranate Slicers* (Spread the Word, 2005); Tolu Ogunlesi: "The Trophy", first appeared in *The Vocabula Review* (January 2007, Vol. 9, No. 1); Grace Nichols: "Icons" from *Sunris* (Virago, 1996); Nii Ayikwei Parkes: "Stripping Yam" was first broadcast on BBC World Service in June 2007, and "E Be So" first appeared in *Wasafiri* (Volume 24 Issue 3, 2009); Janett Plummer: "Red String" from *Lifemarks* (flipped eye publishing, mouthmark series, 2009); Denise Saul: "Scent of Sex" from *White Narcissi*, (flipped eye, 2007); Sudeep Sen: "Almaya, Jaffa" from *The Wolf, Indian Literature*, (Kavya Bharati, 2009) "Winter" first appeared in *The Literary Review, Indian Literature,* (Kavya Bharati, 2009); Seni Seneveratne: "Blood Red Drowning" and "After Qana – July 30 2006" from *Wild Cinnamon and Winter Skin* (Peepal Tree Press, 2007); John Siddique: "Ash Moon" and "Promises" from *Recital – An Almanac* (SALT, 2009); Lemn Sissay: "Winter : Shepherd's Warning" from *Listener* (Canongate, 2008); Dorothea Smartt: "Red Mudder" from *Ship Shape* (Peepal Tree Press, 2008)

RED

AN ANTHOLOGY OF

CONTEMPORARY BLACK BRITISH POETRY

EDITED BY

KWAME DAWES

PEEPAL TREE

First published in Great Britain in 2010
by Inscribe an imprint of
Peepal Tree Press Ltd
17 King's Avenue
Leeds LS6 1QS
UK

ISBN 13: 9781845231293

Supported by
ARTS COUNCIL
ENGLAND

CONTENTS

1

2

3

4

5

6

FOREWORD

"The true colour of life is the colour of the body, the colour of the covered red, the implicit and not explicit red of the living heart and the pulses. It is the modest colour of the unpublished blood." – **Alice Meynell** [British writer, critic, editor, suffragist]

"History could pass for a scarlet text, its jot and title graven red in human blood." – **Eldridge Cleaver** [African-American writer, social critic and radical intellectual]

"We'll no longer sing the sad, despairing spirituals!
Another song will spring forth from our throats
Our red flags we shall unfurl,
Stained by the blood of our upright brothers.
Beneath this sign we shall march,
Beneath this sign we are marching.
Standing tall, the wretched of the earth!
Standing tall, the legions of the hungry!"
– **Jacques Roumain**
[Haitian novelist, poet, anthropologist, politician]

Red is contemporary Black British poetry at the zenith of vibrancy. It is not constant, it is not fixed, it is not static. Just as the colour itself is a signifier that we cannot ignore, whether as an alert to war or warmth, so this fiery collection demands to be noticed. Among over four-score writers featured are many familiar names whose stalwart contribution on the British literary scene goes back decades, along-side others representing the new concerns of a younger generation.

These poets draw on rich heritages from all the world's continents, and without their contribution the literature of Britain would be much the poorer.

Perhaps the most significant thing to be said about *Red* is that the poets in this volume burst through any constraining label with writing that throbs and pulses and seeps and flows. As Kwame Dawes notes in his Preface: "Perhaps it is fair to say that we have now earned the right to produce an anthology that is less about defining Black British identity or announcing its presence and credibility in the literary world, but simply about reminding readers that as poets, Black British poets are ultimately interested in the word and in the joy and challenge of making images and finding music through words."

Those words evoke emotions that are never predictable. Sometimes, as John Agard knows, "one syllable will do / for that river that runs in the veins of all / and washes over tradition and taboo". Sometimes, as for Ebele Ajogbe, the words "bleed sorrow / onto the page". Red can be Moniza Alvi's "sleeping wound", or the initiation of Nii Ayikwei Parkes's homecoming, or the bombast of Faustin Charles's Carnival Robber or Lemn Sissay's tell-tale winter warning. It can be a reminder, as Imtiaz Dharker puts it, "that somewhere I had another land", or Patience Agbabi's insight that "blood and heart mean more than black and white". And in the end, discovers Monika-Akila Richards: "Red makes everything real."

Red embraces life, history, despair and triumph, the everyday and the visionary, encompassing the extremes and differences that contribute to who we are, as well as what we share in common. Black British poetry is indeed moving forward and standing tall.

Full of compelling voices that will not be chilled to silence, spiced with a world view that is the excitement of modern Britain, this unique anthology augurs well for the future – a reading experience to be savoured.

Margaret Busby
London

PREFACE

An artist must be free to choose what he does, certainly, but
he must also never be afraid to do what he must choose.
– Langston Hughes, "The Negro Artist and the Racial Mountain"

Why "Red"? When Kadija Sesay asked me to edit the anthology I knew that I did not want to edit a conventional anthology based on a general call for poems by Black British poets. I felt that there had to be some distinctive quality to the anthology that would allow us to create an interesting and thought-provoking series of images and that would also allow us to make a book that is attractive and unusual. A thematic anthology seemed like a fitting option. More than that, I felt that Black British poetry has now arrived at a place where the pressure to justify itself through works that somehow seek to explain, by theme and focus, what Black Britishness is as an ethnicity can now be resisted. I felt a themed anthology would be intriguing enough to interest and inspire poets to create; it would be broad enough to allow for a varied and diverse series of interpretations and it would avoid the didacticism that telegraphed the need to write about "Blackness". It is my view that the most compelling poems about race and identity do not set out to be about race and identity but to be poems growing out of the poet's need to use language to express the profound experiences of self and soul. So a themed anthology it would be.

I decided against any theme that would lead the poets to imagine that the work was primarily about the meaning of race. The label Black British was enough of a defining factor in that regard and seemed to point to the best instincts of understanding race and culture. So I wanted the poets to stretch a little. I also wanted to

17

create a setting for the anthology that would make the poems feel invested in the shape of the work. It might have been easier to ask for any poem, and then choose the best work I got. But I resisted that since I did not imagine that this was to be a comprehensive accounting of all the card-carrying Black British poets working in the UK today. Instead, I saw this as an exercise that could attract poets who were stirred by the challenge of writing new work along the thematic line suggested. Of course, I was also open to poems that were already composed (and even published) that connected well with the theme "red".

But this still does not explain why "Red". I pulled it out of the proverbial hat. I decided that a colour would be good, though blue would lead to too many poems about the blues, black would lead to too many poems about blackness, and yellow just seemed wrong. Green would trigger some other agenda, and so on. So red. I thought, well, red will connect with passion in that clichéd sense, but it would also allow poets to try to go beyond the cliché. As should be clear, my rationalisation was not extremely profound. I took solace in the idea that red had a lot of possibilities and I wanted to allow for possibilities more than anything else. There is a peculiar irony in the choice of such a theme. One might imagine that having a theme would be restrictive for contributors. But I calculated that for active poets, making a decision about what poems to send for an anthology, when no defining rubric is offered, can be quite daunting. I feared that the first instinct of most poets facing a call for Black British poetry would be to send work that they imagined justified their inclusion in such an anthology. I also imagined that some poets might spend time trying to second guess what kind of work I might be interested in. They might consider my tendency towards the narrative and lyric poem and presume that such work would be more likely to make it into the anthology. And even those poets who consciously resisted such considerations, who were comfortable with sending their "best" work, would still be faced with the dilemma of deciding what to send. I reasoned that an open ended theme like "red" would signal that I was looking first for interesting poems, and that I was not looking for any explicit indication of Black British identity save what might be obvious by their self-identification as such. Thankfully, my calculations were correct.

While we sought to leave the defining of Black British up to the poets themselves – in other words, to the process of self-selection – we did have to think carefully about our use of the phrase as we made a call for poems. The term Black British is an evolving one. I am not sure that anyone can say categorically what it constitutes today. On one hand there are those who simply define Black British as representing any person living in the British Isles who is not Caucasian. This, of course is a fairly broad definition, predicated on the idea of minority status, with some relationship to the term "people of colour". The defining line, one expects, would be discussion around what constitutes Britishness. The other end of the spectrum can be quite limiting even as it has become increasingly articulated as the way to go. Here black is connected almost entirely to Africa, so Black British often refers to British people of African descent.

The history of Black British experience in the UK has made it necessary for us to avoid such limiting definitions because these definitions are quite slippery. After all, what does one do with a West Indian of Indian descent? Surely that person can safely self-identify as Black British. And what does one do with the poet who is not a British citizen but belongs to an migrant or refugee community from Africa? Again, we have chosen to rely on the poets to self-identify. If a poet felt comfortable with the label Black British, then he or she was welcome to submit work to the anthology.

Above everything else, however, the collection is an engaging series of meditations on the idea of red. Sometimes red is the star of the poem, presenting itself in a bold way and driving the whole agenda of the poem. But just as often, the colour is only suggested as a mood or a detail that takes on varied meaning in the context of this anthology.

It is fitting that as its first foray into the Black British anthology, Peepal Tree Press, through its Inscribe imprint, has chosen an innovative way to tackle the anthology. Peepal Tree Press has, in the last few years, strengthened its commitment to the publishing of

Black British writers, adding, in the process, a much needed dimension to its well-established position as the leading publisher of Caribbean Literature today. This anthology represents an important signal of this new adventure. Given the remarkable number of gifted poets emerging in the UK today, and given the work being done by many articulate and proactive advocates for Black British writing in general and poetry in particular, the future looks exciting.

Red, I hope, is a distinctive addition to the strong tradition of anthologies of Black British poetry. Perhaps it is fair to say that we have now earned the right to produce an anthology that is less about defining Black British identity or announcing its presence and credibility in the literary world, and simply about reminding readers that as poets, Black British poets are ultimately interested in the word and in the joy and challenge of making images and finding music through language. The sheer pleasure of this process is what I believe has been captured in these poems. Hopefully, you will agree.

Kwame Dawes
Columbia, SC

If a egg, natty inna di red
Bob Marley

Artists can color the sky red because they know it's blue.
Those of us who aren't artists must color things the way
they really are or people might think we're stupid.
Jules Feiffer

When in doubt wear red.
Bill Blass

1

The hue of the long-wave end of the visible spectrum, evoked in the human observer by radiant energy with wavelengths of approximately 630 to 750 nanometers; any of a group of colors that may vary in lightness and saturation and whose hue resembles that of blood; one of the additive or light primaries; one of the psychological primary hues.

Dictionary.com

1. adjective (redder, reddest) 1. of a colour at the end of the spectrum next to orange and opposite violet, as of blood, fire, or rubies. 2. (of a person's face) red due to embarrassment, anger, or heat. …

OED

ABDULLAHI BOTAN HASSAN "KURWEYNE"

RED

People are not all alike
they're as the fingers on my hand
each person brings what they have
of wisdom and knowledge, and so
let me now expound as much
of what little I know.

Red reaches in different directions
as each side is considered;
we see its various intentions.

When what is spoken of is beauty
it plays a significant role,
it also tells you of slaughter and injury
with drops of coagulated blood;
in a place where danger threatens
it says, "Do not enter!" "Stay away!";
at times it informs, shows
a decision that prevents mishap;
then where a doctor is present
it tells of kindness and help;
when a bride is taken to her home
her fingers are coloured with henna;
the one without a watch
understands its testimony
that night has passed;
the red earth is the sign
that you've crossed from Bari
through the regions of the Haud
have reached the pool of Abudwaaq;
when there's no inflammation,
and the infected wound is healing

then it's tied up with hope;
in his reddened hands
is the sign of the man
who's picked the spring *yi'ib* berries;
when they play football
in stadiums full of fans
except for just sometimes
it's what Arsenal wears.

In a wailing man with welled-up tears
or one consumed with anger
or one who has failed to sleep
your eyes know it,
red appears there.

I have not exhausted
what I know of red
let me finish my speech there
let me leave behind
a sentence in conclusion:
whenever red dries up
it becomes black!

translated from the Somali by Martin Orwin

SYLVIA JEAN ABRAHAMS

TASTING

Mounting the red brick wall, we lean
against scratchy grey bark, on toetips reach up
through unbending branches for the reddest
pomegranates, that snap off, bright
and tough as fresh cricket balls,
though not so round.

We sit, heels kicking, crack leathery skin,
brag our halved fruit along the wall,
suck up juicy sacs – scowl
at tasting red sweet-acid,
that soon sheens our faces rosy-red.

Our cheeks bulging with hard seed,
we spit, aiming for the street,
but hit a passing pale-skin girl,
who snivels and drops her tan school case.
Her brother glares, his hanky's a white flag
swabbing at the rosy-red staining her skirt.

My cousin sticks her tongue out.
We all know they shouldn't be here,
not on our street, when that snotty girl
grabs her brother's hanky, wipes her face,
kneels, clicks the case latch open.

The lid smacks the pavement,
opening up guavas.
A case full of guavas, guavas the size
of my hand, skins of pale green,
though their flesh will only be pinky-yellow,
with tiny pips for slipping down throats.

That girl takes a squelchy bite, as
sweet musk scent seeps, offers
the guava, gashed by her teeth,
and I gasp at its flesh, so tender red,
swap my half a rosy-red pomegranate.

I bite into her sweet tooth marks, tasting
red, and we swap smiles – as her brother
picks up her case, drags her off by the hand.

SHANTA ACHARYA

INFINITY OF RED

Lips   blushing cheeks
colour of magic
hennaed hands and feet
desire blazing like autumnal leaves

Fields of poppies   bouquet of roses
flowers of the *gulmohur* tree   flame of the forest
red hibiscus   fuchsia   peonies
pomegranate seeds scattering like rubies

Red button in the Mandarin's cap
ruby   coral   garnet   rose   quartz   cornelian
red cap   revolutionist   bohemian
red tincture   philosopher's stone
Judas' red hair   Beefeater man
red herring   Red Sea   Red Indian

Red Cross for neutrality
blood banks   children dying of AIDS/HIV
red in heraldry   fortitude & magnanimity
red light   red flag   danger signal
red light district   brothel
caught red handed   red faced like a monkey

Shades of red in earth sky   sunrise sunset
cherries   carrots   chillies   tomatoes   beetroot
red-blooded man   anaemic woman
low haemoglobin   iron   menses
red rags   red capes   bullfights
flags of countries   in the red   bound in red tape
red box of the Chancellor of the Exchequer

Mary in maroon-red and blue   *The Annunciation*
Marilyn Monroe's red dress in *Niagara*
Julia Roberts   *Pretty Woman*   red Ferraris
Benarasi silk saris   Indian weddings
vermillion on the bride's forehead
red bangles   *sankha*   blood on the sheets   red letter day
love letters written in blood   bruises wounds

JOHN AGARD

SONNET #13

This red elixir of a waterfall
over rock of bone. Let's agree to call
it Blood. Yes, Blood. One syllable will do
for that river that runs in the veins of all
and washes over tradition and taboo.

They say the first drop spilled was all it took
to begin the first rose that can pierce thornwise
and seize the heart by passion's hook and crook.
Blood that crowns the sorrow of paradise
and scatters its petals of forgiveness.

See how it leaves its print on history's purest page.
This moon-blessed companion of life and death.
This wine that clings to a common vine of flesh.
See how it stains your cloth of joy as well as rage.

PATIENCE AGBABI

SEEING RED

1.

Black mum parts my continent of head,
with glazed black cotton begins to wind
each division so fiercely my mind
bleeds black. I can't close my eyes in bed.

White mum uses fading wavy thread,
the tension less cruel, more kind
but the vision colour-blind
so I see red.

2.

I read the instructions for shocking-red dye
(freedom has given me the green light)
yet bury the evidence under a head-tie

like the insight
that I see the world through a red eye
where blood and heart mean more than black and white.

FOREIGN EXCHANGE

In Hamburg, me and Anna, who is German,
and a man across the street attacks us, spitting
his violence; the air is cold, and bitter
faces gather like rainclouds, like an omen
and my gentle friend counter-attacks but later
refuses to translate and that's the killer,
her silence, like a shroud; I feel the colour
rage in my cheeks for lack of that translation

reminding me of school, that French exchange,
a simple sentence, *Parce qu'elle est noire*,
delivered at such speed and with such hatred
it hurt me: to encounter so much rage;
more, for being judged solely by colour;
but most, the fact it had to be translated.

COMEDOWN

The mind is its own place, and in itself
Can make a heav'n of hell, a hell of heav'n
                    Milton, *Paradise Lost*

It wasn't the rent boy in Heaven
who looked fifteen and called us dollies,
with his social worker as an accessory
I thought was his boyfriend, leading us up
to the party full of lacklustre women
in tight polyester, and upstairs, not
the Skin with the spider's web tattoo
for a face that bled red light in my skull;
nor the ugly man who said, *Full of fucking*
spades and half-castes as soon as we entered
whom I misheard, the social worker
doing his damnedest to sugar the pill:
it was taking a drug that made us innocent
enough to leave Heaven and end up in Hell.

SOL

After I huffed, puffed, pushed you into the pool
of light and blood on the crushed white sheet
you screamed like an abattoir, like shit,
breaking the day to smithereens until
they swaddled you, our son, our Sol:
you were light, light-skinned, skinny, sugar-sweet,
hair iridescent with blood, eyes bloodshot
but they said they would heal

and they did. Home, we keep you in the shade
in a basket bed where we watch you grow
golden, golden brown, your eyes indigo
to bronze, stare and stare at the ladybird
with a rattle for a heart. All you know
is mum and dad, is black and white, and red.

EBELE AJOGBE

I BLEED

My notepad is my 3rd hand
My pen is my 11th finger
Cut me
and I bleed
  blue
  red
  green
  black
ink
oozing
  spurting
out of my veins

I am Medusa
snakes of poetry
hissing out of my creative dome
Behead me
and my head will roll
and bleed sorrow
onto the page

I am the sacrificial lamb
at the altar ego of my human self
eyes dead open
tongue hanging out
swollen
from too many thoughts
unspoken

Heavily pregnant
labour's setting in
my water's just broke

and I'm gushing
pushing
bleeding
  blue
  red
  green
  black
ink

Nurse!
Quick!
Please!
Pass me a notepad
Pass me a pen
'cos like it or not
this baby is coming OUT

If it's a boy,
I'll call him Copyright
If it's a girl,
I'll call her All Rights Reserved
('cos I reserve the right
to bleed onto the page
in any colour I choose)

My notepad is my 3rd hand
My pen is my 11th finger

Cut me
and don't stem the flow

I want to bleed

…so I'm gonna bleed

I want to bleed me a rainbow.

EXODUS

baby
moses
cries

dies
between
africa's
thighs

the nile
flows
menstrual

MIR MAHFUZ ALI

"DAD, WHY ARE ROSES RED?"

My son must think
I know about everything.
Sitting on my lap, he asks,
"Dad, why are roses red?"
Even before he hears me
his face gleams with satisfaction.
I scratch my chin
and watch his handsome face.
Only my son can look like this.
How can I disappoint him now?
I can tell him
how the smell of roses
can travel far in the sky.
Or how we fear their thorns.
He might give up on me
if I don't come out with a story.
But I say nothing.
Then something dances inside me.

Roses used to be white
like the infinite snow in Siberia
but one day when a dove
flew over a garden
the air smelled of the attar
with which Gods washed their feet.
The dove looked in the direction
of the sweet aroma
and saw the roses blooming.
Each flower had a beautiful eye
like a star above an exile.
The bird fell in love with the roses.
In a trance it flew

to perch on a branch.
The thorn did what it does best
when someone comes
to take its flower.
It pierced the bird's soft breast.
It fluttered its wings
to free itself from feeling larger
than its own life,
covered the white roses with the scarlet
that seeped through its snowy feathers.
They melt just long enough
to colour the flowers red
from petal to petal, first
with slow trickles then quickly.
At evening the dove cooed
to the flowers for the last time,
"I am your blood".

This is why we have red roses.

MONIZA ALVI

THE SLEEPING WOUND

Hush, do not waken
the sleeping wound.

It lies on its crimson pillow,
red against red.

The long wound in the afternoon.
The long wound in the evening.

Centuries later,
no longer red,

it opens its eyes
at the most tentative kiss.

BIBI

WHEN I THINK OF

We have loved with such intensity,
We are scalded by passion.

———————————

Life pressed in the heart of Love poured into
A clay cup and offered to the thirsty.

———————————

He was blistered by lust
And
Pockmarked by the absence of love.

———————————

Love lay asleep smouldering beneath a bed
Of bittersweet embers; she spied my desire and began to rise.

MAROULA BLADES

BLOOD ORANGE

At Kiang-Nan in the Kiangsu
There are small scarlet oranges
That the winter doesn't kill
Because the air is truly sweet at Kiang-Nan.
                    (Eighth century Chinese poem. Author unknown.)

I'm an orange bandit in a thick scarf.
Bloody is my flesh, it's sour to kiss,
But it's plump with good things to stain lips.

Unzip my organza négligée
To release a lachrymal heart,
I'll tease and colour you quietly.

On the sapphire Indian Ocean,
Forefathers' skins were etched by salt,
Naked they bled riding petticoat waves.

Our home was a dhow from Kiang-Nan
Where words of love rolled amid cannon and ball,
The rhythmic squall softened a sailor's heart,

He stole away in a boat filled with hessian sacks
And planted new orchards in distant lands
Where our blood became sweeter and sweeter.

We have liberty now stamped red on our skins,
Symbiotic we are with the new vine and earth,
Our tongues are narrow, but the blood swells rich.

I'm an infidel swiftly diminishing,
Precious oils have dried in wells,
I'm all chewed up inside, I know it.

This once sexy bandit's belly button's black.
I'm a host for egg-laying strangers.
Come to my bowl, tease cerise, taste my tang.

It's too late, hand; I'm really rotten now.

TROPICAL HEAT

Ribbons of water spin brown sago leaves,
Flies blur the reflection of the mango trees,
A fog of secrets rises in the humid air.
It's the hunger season where evil spirits tread,
Snaking between the debris of bleached bones,
Even the rotten fish heads look possessed
With beady eyes drying on the riverbed.
Along the parched banks sepia skulls lie;

Bees sweep in the void of the ghost snares,
Ants march in the shade of a spade-shaped stone,
Parrots riot above as the sun sinks low,
An emotional fade lingers overhead,
Rising to fall like sharp notes off the horizon.
Wings make strange figurations sky-high,
Lizards circle to lick the lazuli skies.
Frogs break across soil like an oil slick;

A herd of happenings rush by the green.
Cold poverty moans over this torrid heat.
A lean child forms cones from a large leaf,
Filters water, drinks and swallows a leech.
Skin burns and the mind is dense like peat.
And sleep is like an estranged mate, seeking.
Drums tighten and crack; the reds fade away,
As cinnamon pearls spill through the twilight.

MALIKA BOOKER

FADED SLIPPERS

Your son lives across town with his mother.
Each nightly visit, I slip my feet into his red Snoopy slippers,
a perfect fit, the way I want to fit you,
long to slide me into your life.
There is no room for me here.

Our late night conversations till 5 am,
our bodies writhing your cool sheets,
our arms wrapping each other in sleep
mean nothing
except
a moment to add to strings of moments
whose names reside in your little black book.

I am a single man having fun, you say,
your smile hinting of other bodies
tangled in your bed sheets, on other nights.
Women who want to stay, too.

Each caress, phone call,
I want to crawl into you more,
snuggle like my feet in his slippers.

That night you played ballads, waltzing me for hours.
Gliding in those slippers, dreams whispered possibilities;
something fluttered.
I wanted to be more than a moment, a black book woman;
Scalded by your indifference, I felt scarlet in that shuffle.
Some nights, memories of that dance spill onto my lonely pillow.

CEMENT

Last week my tears dried up,
the water sucked out with our aborted child.
Yesterday in the shower, pain contorted,
I squatted, expelled a souvenir
red, liver textured, squeezed out.
I scornfully scooped and flushed it away.
Where were you?

Your gritty words no longer make me cry,
my tears are gone, so I plaster my heart
against your every grit-worrying wound
each layer cementing thicker concrete.

Now I understand older black women like my aunts,
their hard posture. Why I never saw them cry.
My father made my mother stony, a martyr for her kids,
brittle and bitter, till my step-dad unpicked her stones.
Layer by layer, I watched her walls crumble until she mellowed.

My aunt, shattered by fists, blocked her heart
stone cold, her tears withered.
All my life I never saw her cry, until foetal
in a hospital bed, wrapped in my mother's arms,
facing death, tears tracking her face she whispered, *I am scared.*
Crying for all her tear-barren years.

Washing water-diluted blood down the drain,
bleaching the bath tiles white, I want to crumple,
bawl my eyes out, but I have learnt my lesson well.
Each passing day hardens my voice. I am becoming a wall,
barbed wire protecting concrete too tough to shatter.
Concrete protecting heart too tender to bare.
It's too late for me.

MARK ANGELO DE BRITO

UNITY

for Gro Mambo Angela

Mali Loui,
divine rebel in your head,
your message was healing,
was unity,
that those who keep faith
with lwa and orisha
must rise and walk as one,
if the house will hold
against others' assault
or rift within.

You invoked a unity
of now
and common struggle,
not subservient
to place or past.

"But," they said,
the detractors,
kneelers before nation,
"what unity is there
but return
to root of Africa,
beyond graft and corruption?"

They do not see
that *Ginen* is another Africa
we will visit only,
living or dead,
through soul's journey

across the waters:
a calabash conveys us
to the realm of gods
and ancestors.

Tradition is not
one man's
improvisation,
but the striving of all
towards voice of the divine,
in tune with time
and circumstance:
we do not need another
empire's denial
of five hundred years.

Perhaps it is the Gede
alone
can resolve our twisted
ancestry of rape
and accident
to destined wholeness.

"A sea of blood frames
the tradition:
many have died for the truth
of these religions.
I am the lwa set Haiti free,
at a time when slavery
was all over the world."

Mali Loui,
creole goddess,
armed with all the fury
of Petro,

I call on you as guide
in the paths of fate
and struggle,
our strength before,
and now again.

FAUSTIN CHARLES

THE RED ROBBER

From the depths of burning Hell
I came
Cast out because I rape Satan's daughter
My rage is a millionfold
My mother was a dragon
And my father a griffin
I can drink a river
And belch an ocean
When my name is called in vain
My belly blows rain
Flooding villages, towns, and cities
I eat countries boiled in vinegar
Emperors and kings tremble
At the sound of my name
Snakes hiss! Wolves howl!
Volcanoes split fire exploding
Damnation scattering the sun
Watch me
As I devour these islands
Watch me
As I drink the Caribbean Sea
Brainwashing minds hatched
From a rotten egg, circling
The plague-ridden universe
I was the conqueror, slave-driver
And slave
My body grew in the passing
Of centuries
I can destroy
And I can create
Watch me
Reshaping islands from sea-spray
Sweat and grass.

51

A MASQUERADER FASHIONS RED AT CARNIVAL NIGHT

Flowers to red fire feed
The blood of the hours bleed
Sunset lighting the red light
Of coming moonlight
Flames dress the feast
Where the crimson masks of every beast
Strikes sparks to burn away
The dangers of night and day;
A scarlet face grins vermillion
And spins red eyes through black x-ray vision.

DEBJANI CHATTERJEE

FIRE

Explosion of flame-in-the-forest blooms,
my myriad tongues lacerate the sky,
my crimson face forever bears witness –
I flare, I splutter, seemingly I die.

In my flamboyance pure lightning flowers –
I am both Sacrifice and Predator.
Primeval bridge between people and gods,
Heaven and Earth cannot hold my splendour.

Worshippers offer me ghee oblations
I seal the ties of treaties and weddings
and at life's end I am the warm embrace
that speeds the soul to its final resting.

My many forms are fickle and diverse;
immortal, I consume the universe.

CREMATION GHAT

A scarlet sari
flutters in the saffron sky
above a blazing pyre.

As in a dream, a spectre rises;
all sound is cremated.
In mute persistence, a jackal waits.

MAYA CHOWDHRY

KALI MIRCHI

kali mirchi predicts the fall of nations
pursuing a palatable future
in the Malabar mangroves

her emerging flower spike
ripening red, climbing the coffee crop
blackened skin abraded to white
to pepper a jar of Pataks

SPURN

he monitored her via her handbag
unearthing forbidden tampons
she crept with blood-congealed thighs
stalking the cornershop for *Always Ultra*

he threw the unclean khanna heart-ward;
boiling masala sticking her kameez to her
she held her scream even as pani cascaded
soaking her shedding skin

he improvised his strikes on her
and afterwards he made sure
she played snakes and ladders
afraid to throw the dice

for fear of winning and being
plunged back in the snake-pit

JOSEPH COELHO

RED ROSE

Tiptoeing over the shards of another day,
feet covered in safflower oil,
Ben wonders if red tinted glasses are better than rose.

Scarred legs slip and get cut through the night.
A mother's words blossom on the skin
like bruises in a creased rose.

Stumbling with a wounded outlook,
he wonders what edgy word will smash tomorrow,
what scab will be pierced by a thorn from his mother's rose.

The cuts in his eyes never get space to heal.
Blood stains the white around his irises.
Ben wonders if her red eyes were once also rose.

FRED D'AGUIAR

THE NEVER-NEVER

Never our bodies lit by a lamp whose wick
Shoulders an oil snake for a flame
Licking soot onto the glass lamp
Casting a shadow diluted orange
As the slow burn of your kiss would have it
As my memory insists upon pitching it

And never the old cartwheel on one spot
Repeated until the eyes revolve in the head
And the earth-spin takes on a caterwauling
Laying the fine hairs in my inner ear flat
As I am laid out on my willing back
As my back flattens itself on the earth's map

Never the owl whose eye centres a storm
And the storm that mimics a star's fall
For breeze kills that oil lamp
Leaves one big shadow for a world
As I am there with you and both of us
As twins in that dark that fuses us

Never a book opened for anything
But reprimand and nothing but rules
In any book worth opening or so it seemed
Waist-high with things that gripped me
As a wave grips the sea and sea grips sand
As a current runs through the sky's open hand

MARTIN DE MELLO

OCTOBER 19

beech leaves tend not to go yellow
rose hips, an oak nearly dead
on its leaves thousands of silk button galls

willowherb a series in pink
clouds near the end blushing red
papery skeletons of hogweed

tall grass and thistle
not all of the sun made of cobwebs

2

so much depends
upon

a red wheel
barrow

glazed with rain
water

beside the white
chickens.

William Carlos Williams

He did not wear his scarlet coat,
For blood and wine are red,
And blood and wine were on his hands
When they found him with the dead,
The poor dead woman whom he loved,
And murdered in her bed.

Oscar Wilde

IMTIAZ DHARKER

HOW TO CUT A POMEGRANATE

"Never," said my father,
"never cut a pomegranate
through the heart. It will weep blood.
Treat it delicately, with respect.

Just slit the upper skin across four quarters.
This is a magic fruit,
so when you split it open, be prepared
for the jewels of the world to tumble out,
more precious than garnets,
more lustrous than rubies,
lit as if from inside.
Each jewel contains a living seed.
Separate one crystal.
Hold it up to catch the light.
Inside is a whole universe.
No common jewel can give you this."

Afterwards, I tried to make necklaces
of pomegranate seeds.
The juice spurted out, bright crimson,
and stained my fingers, then my mouth.

I didn't mind. The juice tasted of gardens
I had never seen, voluptuous
with myrtle, lemon, jasmine,
and alive with parrots' wings.

The pomegranate reminded me
that somewhere I had another home.

LIZZY DIJEH

MOTHER
(photographed in 1977)

My Virgin Mary,
all pretty in pink
standing mantle-tall,
red carpet-treated and Bosch-flamed.

I do not know that skin-thin girl,
that beautiful, all-cocoa glow,
beaming through that satin silk, that Western milk
pulsing through red-blooded veins,

all shimmering, shining, sequins winking
before the gas-fuelled instrument, Ibo-less.
I do not know those painted lips, those pink hips,
those Rhine-lines that could challenge the Niger divide,

those strapped heels that rise and rise
on platforms Hausa-high,
to breach a silent wall that preaches blushingly
in twenty-five different languages.

I learnt later that father had carefully snuck away
behind the frame, out of sight,
to capture his quasi-English rose, his bride-to-be,
to bind her up, to tie her down,

and I wanted to scream at my mirror, my size-10 grin,
warn her of the danger ahead:

The furry Red Sea that gathers
like locusts around her feet,
the Beatle-heat that creeps and creeps
to threaten those satin sheets.

I have studied Hamlet,
I know the drill, how families kill
twenty-five times in twenty-five years
in twenty-five different languages.

I notice Lennon hovering,
her girlhood idol, her Mr *All-you-need-is-love*
and watch him muffle something inaudible in her ear.
The words fly white and lightly home.

Of course she does not see a husband
behind the Kodak lens, the man he will be,
the dumb-bell
weight

of the four string of ropes that will cast a noose
each year around her neck, the quartet of Sumo-tonsils
who will wrestle like drunks forged and forced from a pub,
all-loud, all-wanting dissidents

pushed into this world
all-breaking chords
whilst kick-boxing their bloody way
past each of her sweaty knees.

In a single flash she has become
transfixed, transformed, un-flinched, un-scared,
bound and tied, staring hard and wide-eyed
at her future.

It is not me she sees,
her mirror, *her* beautiful babe
from a post-Lennon age staring right back,
un-bound, un-tied,

yelling, yelling
in an awkward, all-loud and all-demanding tone:
Mum, Mother, Mummy –
get thee to a Nunnery, go!

SUNDAY IGBO-ISM

There will be talk of a reunion, a testament to Eden
as the red cloth is fed with Christmas.

He will set himself down between his buoys
and prepare to take his great big bow at the head

of our Buddha chop-shop, our mesh of flesh,
our cupped bowl of brown legs and brown breasts,

heaving and steaming off the blind bone, pouring, adoring
at those skinned and pinned in by a fine maternal grasp

of stained glass, tamed holly and season.

One by one our heads will sink like pink bowling balls
at the sounds of Moses and Noah swimming in our Red Sea,

our chins will fill with iron-lead and sink and sink
with the Almighty weight of such shut gates.

Mine will roll as far as Adam's apple,
his collarbone, taut, tough and busy in spots,

mine will feel all light at the site,
without a trace, without a taste of white,

prepare to take my great big bite, and dare to let
my dark balloons rise and rise like kites.

TISHANI DOSHI

HOMECOMING

I forgot how Madras loves noise –
Loves neighbours and pregnant women
And gods and babies

And Brahmins who rise
Like fire hymns to sear the air
With habitual earthquakes.

How funeral processions clatter
Down streets with drums and rose-petals,
Dancing death into deafness.

How vendors and cats make noises
Of love on bedroom walls and alleyways
Of night, operatic and dark.

How cars in reverse sing *Jingle Bells*
And scooters have larynxes of lorries.
How even colour can never be quiet.

How fisherwomen in screaming red –
With skirts and incandescent third eyes
And bangles like rasping planets –

And Tamil women on their morning walks
In saris and jasmine and trainers
Can shred the day and all its skinny silences.

I forgot how a man dying under the body
Of a tattered boat can ask for promises;
How they can be as soundless as the sea

On a wounded day, altering the ground
Of the earth as simply as the sun filtering through –
The monsoon rain dividing everything.

ODE TO THE WALKING WOMAN

After Alberto Giacometti

Sit —
you must be tired
of walking,
of losing yourself
this way:
a bronzed rib
of exhaustion
thinned out
against the dark.
Sit —
there are still things
to believe in;
like civilisations
and birthing
and love.
And ancestors
who move
like silent tributaries
from red-earthed villages
with history cradled
in their mythical arms.
But listen,
what if they swell
through the gates
of your glistening city?
Will you walk down
to the water's edge,
immerse your feet
so you can feel them
dancing underneath?
Mohenjodaro's brassy girls
with bangled wrists

and cinnabar lips;
turbaned Harappan mothers
standing wide
on terracotta legs;
egg-breasted Artemis –
Inana, Isthar, Cybele,
clutching their bounteous hearts
in the unrepentant dark,
crying: *Daughter,*
where have the granaries
and great baths disappeared?
Won't you resurrect yourself,
make love to the sky,
reclaim the world?

SUNRISE AT SANCHI STUPA

after W.S. Merwin

"O fire, thou art the son of heaven by the body of earth."
– *Rig Veda* Book III, Hymn XXV

We were sitting outside the stupa that morning when the sun shone
down like a woman sweeping clear roads of dust
and dreams making me wonder if love can find its way like this
through broken valleys past shattered edge of bramble
thorn and bruised foundation of monastery All-conquering love
doesn't stir in the dark to talk to guards
doesn't have the quietness of cows doesn't run with incensed rage
across the bougainvillea fringe of the world
If love were really born of fire we'd build giant domes of sky
around our gossiping pasts and silence them
with bits of tooth or graft of hoary nail we'd let the road consume
our steps our columns of desire
and when morning broke the scattering earth with blood red
points of light all the distances of night
would brush us by as the undergrowth of our unfinished lives

JEANNE ELLIN

BLOOD-RED TO SPICE-RED

Red-raw recruits find butchered-beef feet tenderised by marching.
Squaddies' beetroot necks sweat-washed. Soldiers with grape-vine eyes
drink to forget the red-rags of rebels shot from guns after the mutiny.

Drink to forget their hands, wrist-deep-dyed in the spurt and flow.
Blind-beast-drunks forget that stale raw meat-smell of seeping wounds.
Cayenne of infection draws the fat foreign flies like raspberry jam.

Below their empire apple-red-skin coats they roast under a blinding
chilli sun that must never set on these overgrown children of rain
trudging foreign dust, thirsting, obeying, marching, dying to dye the map.

They turn their coats to khaki, the map fades to pink blancmange. Now
remembrance is not in poppies, but in spices. Profit from dust where
margins are low, lower when you reach that little man who grinds the spice,

thinks of their rich red lives many deals away and so he adds a pinch profit
for himself. Why not Sudan? That uncalculated dose becomes red alert,
flows into reddened lips, gullets, guts, dyeing cells to an unnatural shade.

CRISTA ERMIYA

THREE DAYS RED

On the first day you didn't call.
I poured red wine
over the reputations of my friends.

On the second day, you didn't call.
I sowed poppies
in the furrows of a rival's face.

On the third day, when you didn't call,
I wrote down your still-breathing name
with red ink in a Book of the Dead.

AGNES

Sister Agnes pops prescription pills,
lolls in the kitchen in her swollen skin,

watches the clock.
Her next dose is due. She rises,

resets the clock,
waits quietly for Judgement Day.

Her heart is a lost red balloon
receding into an unfathomable sky.

BERNARDINE EVARISTO

REVENGE

1

Normal

Hardeep
took the Central Line

from Northolt
to Mile End, weekdays,

shuffling through the barriers
in hooded sweatshirt,

rucksack on his back
bulging with books.

He slunk into a seat,
knees splayed out,

Bangra beats
throbbing in his MP3

and glowered
out the window

in an early morning
grump, dreading

a 3 hour lecture
on algorithms at 9 o'clock,

until the train entered
the darkness

at White City
and crowds of commuters

got on
and gobbled him up.

2

Abnormal

Smooth
supertall temples

of the Twentieth, rocking
the island's

skyline.
Arms in totemic supplication

to the God of Microchip,
until the beak

of a small, single-minded bird
pierces the buffed

steel-rodded sides
where it hurts

most
and the walls come a-

tumbling down
and a terrible, untameable,

unforgettable pall
blackens

the island
with apocalyptic ash,

and we cannot believe
what has happened.

3

Mortal

Out of
the mushroomed

cloud,
we see

The Falling Ones –
helpless, high-diving

acrobatics,
head over heels,

so light, so small,
until

crash landed,
a crimson stew of sinew

and ruptured organs –
unrecognisable,

a pulped, smashed-boned
mess.

All in all, nearly 3000.
Dead.

4

Moral

Hardeep
likes old-school hip hop,

Eastenders, cricket,
(Bollywood classics crack him up),

Big Macs, Adidas (not Nike),
Playstation.

One day he'll
move back up North

where his roots are,
he reckons.

That evening
he was glued to the telly,

appalled:
the flaming towers,

the flaming people,
his flaming heart.

It was like a blockbuster
disaster movie, he thought,

only this time
for real.

5

Outrage

Because this day
the lives

of each and every one
of the 6.6 billion people

on earth
had changed forever,

(we were told),
war was declared on Terror –

although no one knew
what it looked like,

exactly.
The Great Leader

discovered
a pipeline to God, suddenly,

who whispered,
"You, my Emissary on Earth,

will henceforth
murder, steal, bear false witness

and use my name
in vain.

Burn the skin of 'em, My Son,
with nitroglycerin.

So let it be written.
Amen."

6

Rage

In the name of Good
we destroy

Evil Forces
in the guise of little girls

and boys
playing in the village dust

and pregnant women
at checkpoints

and whole sleeping towns
in the desert

getting up to the dangerous
business

of sleeping, not a single
house left intact.

From the screens in our cosy
suburban homes

we hear of
carpet bombing,

coalition raids, mortar and rocket
attacks on

"fully legitimate targets",
six figures worth of civilian corpses,

and counting,
millions more dislocated,

"regrettably" –
their sacrifice, not ours

in the fight against
Evil.

7

Damage

Hardeep
takes the Central Line

later than usual
to avoid the crowds

who avoid the spaces
either side

of him, so that sitting isolated
his face burns.

He carries his books
in a transparent plastic bag,

wears his hood down.
No one does anything

except scowl
but when he gets up

fear shivers through
the carriage

like an electric charge;
grown men shoulder

him
like he's an enemy alien

and he wants to shout out,
"I'm Sikh, you tossers."

8

Damnation

In our crusade
to control the glutinous black

juice that greases
our noble civilisation

we toppled the monolith
of absolute power

so that his concrete skull
crashed to the ground.

Yet
we replaced it

with the chaos of car bombs
instead.

Nor had we come home
by Christmas,

brandishing
a bottle of champagne,

at the picket fence,
as expected.

Here
we made one religion

synonymous with terrorism:
imprisoned, tortured, accused —

sowing more seeds
of revenge.

PATRICIA FOSTER

OPEN WOUND

She read about Feng Shui
and bedroom walls painted rose red,

felicitous enhancer and cure
for her and a future lover.

Five years on, the wallpaper buckles,
her bedroom walls uneven to touch,

and where the light barely reaches,
the walls are the colour of a wound.

THE WITNESS

Through the crack of the bedroom door
my father, his voice barking.
My mother's sullen lips refuse
to kiss him sometimes and her stubborn mouth resists
the pull and drag of worn lipstick:
pieces of congealed wax and fat break up
and fall to the floor.
My father's slow and heavy
now, as he moves towards my mother
treading wine-coloured fragments
into the tan carpet, leaving an evident stain.

RED HIBISCUS

Outside the hectare of marsh land, in the rain
a week ago, was a field of summer lavender;
the perfume now dampened and snuffed out.

Beside it, the small lake, spattered
with rain; silver shrapnel piercing the film
of green algae.

On the news this evening
another British soldier is scattered across an Iraqi field
like pollen from the head of a red hibiscus.

JEAN HALL

GRANDMA CLARICE RED DOORSTEP

Grandma Clarice
red doorstep
fi guide heal
and protect
wid voudoun
libation
and much
respect
pass thru
earth bound
connection
wid di
living spirit,
blood
ancestral,
mix
wid
clay
mortar
brick,
come wid
de
head-tie
gabardine
wet
water rag
polish and
spit.

MAGGIE HARRIS

ANOTHER SONG FOR DADDY

1

That girl in St Lucia recognising me –
"Red girl!"
(The nose and mouth? The Guyanese bangles?)

In my longing my heart flipped like a monitor –
in all this Caribbean Sea
this island girl should know
we shared a history

and even on the sailing ship
I walked the plank between
the black boys on the rigging
and the tourists' bright white teeth.

2

There is nothing like a red ant bite
that sharp recognisable sting
that has you jumping up in rage
beating the back of your skirt
like one possessed

and you don't know which is worse –
that you be condemned to hell
by one so small, or lose your cool
in front of posh girls
one hot school afternoon

3

But bring me a bag of peppers
and I'll tell you their names –
piri-piri and pimento
jalopeno, chilli, capsicum –
the smallest always the hottest: bird pepper
lingering at the back of your throat
small guns blazing
refusing to be extinguished
by mere water

4

And should I even attempt to speak
of hibiscus petals
scarlet as that fever
that bore her to her death
as flushed as a new poem
on its way to becoming?

Or of birds whose very plumage
is their undoing
gracing hats and quills,
collectors' glass boxes,
disappearing into graveyards
they christened
museums?

5

All this you must know,

up with the dawn of a Berbice morning
navigating the arteries of rivers

you sail into the foreday morning of my sleep
just as you steered *The Manhattan, The Radio City,*
The Maracaibo

down that river like a king
past abandoned plantations with the most beautiful of names
Lilienberg, Catherine ...
your birthplace Fort Nassau ... aye, aye!

your bauxite cargo pyramids
glowing from flat-bottomed barges

I don't know what you knew of alchemy,
that process that turned that red dust into metal
aluminium, hulls, tin foil

only that
you emerge from beneath the canopy of trees
themselves bleeding

> *hard to believe that trees like these*
> *are trembling far below their knees*
> *on anklebones the hue of stones*
> *and toenails clutching crumbling earth*
> *and water mangrove world*

and a river tired of rinsing her brown hands clean

but what was on your mind but the pay check
your four daughters, your wife
school uniforms, the light bill
a bottle of XM rum?

6

Between that red dust and I
swim one river, one sea, one ocean
and innumerable lives
intersecting, breaking away into tributaries
migrating flat-footed people
from green continents into cities

7

Do you remember that year, 1965,
they gave me a scholarship,
The Reynolds Metals Company
to that posh Georgetown school where
my tongue swelled up and refused me
the liberty of speaking?

8

you
so proud

emerging from the rainforest
in tin-can glory

knowing about sandbanks waiting beneath the tides
kerosene lamps swinging in a red-eye dust
seeing with your far-eye

one Captain, *Aye*
black man/red man emerging
from that core
that beating, pulsing core
of darkness.

LOUISE HERCULES

SCARLET

As you sculpt your supple locks into an ample crest
I keep one eye on you and the other on the hope that you'll join me

Take rest from your tireless task to let each dappled vine
Spill from the chalice of your mane like tamarind husks descending

Descending among you, descending upon me
Until I shall wear them like garlands

Sun blushed & coiled neatly around the ashen canvas of
Bare foot & wrist in a poultice of relic twine

A crush of crimson flex that quickens my slackened pulse within
Two beats of my instinct to think

To sink deeper into the thickets bare till I'm nothing but
A school of silver fish now

Piercing through cutlets of lobe and brow as I too
Become estranged into your swarm.

3

He liked to observe emotions; they were like red lanterns strung along the dark unknown of another's personality, marking vulnerable points.

Ayn Rand

Borders are scratched across the hearts of men, by strangers with a calm, judicial pen, and when the borders bleed we watch with dread the lines of ink along the map turn red

Marya Mannes

Her loved companion, quivering, dead,
His dear wings with his lifeblood red;
And for her golden crested mate
She mourned, and was disconsolate.

Ramayana

CYRIL HUSBANDS

BLOODED

Red…
Mist: my rage consumes, swirls
around me, not the colour of boiling blood
but vivid scarlet, righteously
illuminating lies, injustice, corruption
and hypocrisy; replenishing,
energising my daily struggles

Curtain: velvet opulence, sensuous
alluring, trashily glamorous, hiding
or distracting from sins with its
burlesque, razzle-dazzle presence
the original good-time drape

Eyes: weary, inundated dryness; sore
raw, swollen from the overflow of
emotion from the soul they are the
windows to; flaunting private grief
like so much dirty linen, stained
with fears realised;
pain that can't be considered

Red: a wholesome, satisfyingly addictive
taste of Ghana, of home; black-eyed peas,
palm oil, fierce chillies, plantain
and the essential, magical ingredients of
love, family, deep abiding joy in
lovingly preparing and sharing
food, ritual and company

Dust: desiccated ancestral blood
the land's dry weeping for sins
against us by many, not least
ourselves, a constant reminder that
the land does not belong to us
for the reverse is true; making no
distinction between the expensive hems
of the rich and the bare feet of the poor

Skies: birthing and extinguishing each day
nature showing off the ease
with which she creates splendour
gently, beautifully and emphatically
putting us in our place, arrogant in her
knowledge that we can never truly capture or
recreate her daily miracles

Tongue: an emblem of childhood;
sticky, messy, funny and fondly
remembered; stuck out for the
world to share, to revel in the
owners' good luck; part of a
set that included faces, fingers
and stained clothes

KHADIJAH IBRAHIIM

WHEN MY TIME COME

The Lord is my shepherd, I shall not want.
He makes me lie down in green pastures.
                              Psalm 23

Mi dear chile,
we are livin' in our last days
so when mi time come,
I waant to be buried in mi red suit,
the one I just buy.

I buy a new one every five years
just for de occasion,
I like to keep with the fashion
and dis suit favour de roses in mi garden;
you know how I love dem so.

So look here, child,
when mi time come, I waant you
to remember
dis is de suit I waant to be buried in,
de red one right here,
trailing from neck to hem
wid beads and silk embroidery
just like royalty,
a colour of importance,
I see de queen wearing one just like it pon TV.

So remember what mi show you;
see how it tailor stitched in and
out with good threads,
like mi granny use to do.
She bury in red, too.

And when de Lord calls
I want to be wearing a red suit,
de one I hand pick especially –
I walk de whole day till carn bun mi toes.

I like to look good at all times;
no-one is going to say
I never dress away till de end of my days.
Mi buy mi suit from Marks and Spencer,
all mi underwear, too;
put dem in me trunk
with all mi fine nightwear and tings,
fold in camphor balls.
Mi a ole woman, 75 years just gone,
but mi a no fool;
mi make all mi plans,
put down insurance
fe horse-drawn carriage,
gospel singers, saxophone player,
and a red rose for each and everyone.

Mi no waant bury a Englan',
mi waant mi ashes spread cross de River
Thames, make de wave tek
mi back to which part mi did come from.

And when all and sundries come to de house,
start dig, stake claim to what dem waant,
to what dem no waant,
when tears flare and tongues clash difference,
I want mi daughter to remember
dis is the red suit I waant to be buried in;

the red one right here.

JOSHUA IDEHEN

RED CIRCLE

Blood falling at a right
Angle will always pro
Duce the perfect red
Circle,

Red Circle
Red Circle
She loved the
Red Circle

Muedrigos, he
Was her shield
Against the loneli
Ness of London
Versus the cold
And the callous
Ness It was he
She caught Zs
With at night
It was he, she
Made her WhY
She woke up
Every morning
Here he was her
EX
Had left for
A nicer pair
Of Nipples

Something about
Being alone the
Room is extra chilly

There's even less
On television friends
Either don't exist
Or didn't wait for
You to return their call
No one
Calls you and you
Want no one to call
You want him to
Call you and he
Won't work won't
Save your mood
One night stands muck
And dirty up Your
Feelings, healings
So slow can she feel
It. No she can't
Time is taking its
Time and sometimes
She can't even cry
Just sigh by the TV on
Titanic on BBC One
London can be a bitter
Experience
And slowly she fumbles
The world around her
Crumbles

The man in the shop
Is Turkish, thinks its
Funny calling her Natasha
Beddingfield she can only
Hear the bed-in-field
Plus his here ever
Wanting smirk
Makes her feel more

Sick inside hurry fast
And buy the sharpness
The sharpness home
To the bathroom
With the sharpness

Run a bath, leave a self
Indulgent text saying
She wished she was as
Strong as he
Fuck that no,
No she wished
She had
Found someone to dump
Him first for

                                 snip-

Snip

One razor
No pleasure
Turning purple
This is her   Now
Watching
The red circle
Fall.

LINTON KWESI JOHNSON

FIVE NIGHTS OF BLEEDING
(for Leroy Harris)

1

madness... madness...
madness tight on the heads of the rebels
the bitterness erupts like a hot-blast
                                broke glass
rituals of blood on the burning
served by a cruel in-fighting
five nights of horror an of bleeding
                                broke glass
cold blades as sharp as the eyes of hate
an the stabbings
it's war amongst the rebels
madness... madness... war.

2

night number one was in brixton
soprano B sound system
was a beating out a rhythm with a fire
coming doun his reggae-reggae wire
it was a soun shaking doun your spinal column
a bad music tearing up your flesh
an the rebels them start a fighting
the yout them jus turn wild
it's war amongst the rebels
madness... madness... war.

3

night number two doun at shepherd's
right up railton road

it was a night named Friday
when everyone was high on brew
or drew a pound or two worth a kally
soun coming doun neville king's music iron
the rhythm jus bubbling an back-firing
raging an rising, then suddenly the music cut
steel blade drinking blood in darkness
it's war amongst the rebels
madness... madness... war.

4
night number three
over the river
right outside the rainbow
inside james brown was screaming soul
outside the rebels were freezing cold
babylonian tyrants descended
pounced on the brothers who were bold
so with a flick
of the wrist
a jab an a stab
the song of blades was sounded
the bile of oppresson was vomited
an two policemen wounded
righteous righteous war.

5
night number four at a blues dance
                    a blues dance
two rooms packed an the pressure pushing up
hot. hot heads. ritual of blood in a blues dance
                              broke glass
splintering fire, axes, blades, brain-blast
rebellion rushing doun the wrong road

storm blowing doun the wrong tree
an leroy bleeds near death on the fourth night
                              in a blues dance
on a black rebellious night
it's war amongst the rebels
madness... madness... war.

6
night number five at the telegraph
vengeance walked through the doors
so slow
so smooth
so tight an ripe an smash!
                              broke glass
a bottle finds a head
an the shell of the fire-hurt cracks
the victim feels fear
            finds hands
            holds knife
            finds throat
o the stabbings an the bleeding an the blood
it's war amongst the rebels
madness... madness... war.

ANTHONY JOSEPH

BOUGAINVILLEA: SUPER 8 RED

We spew ourselves up, but already underneath
laughter can be heard.
        – Frantz Fanon, *The Wretched of the Earth*

The road make to walk
on carnival day
        – Lord Kitchener

king carnival
        yuh headpiece so heavy
    so slow to walk
        with this
                costume behind
        as if it built with
                you in it

        midday near memorial park
                in such merciless heat
and these blue hills
        that rim the city
    truck borne
                sound
        of icarian trumpets
a ream of horns
    a rhythm section
        beats iron into
                sound

        ox blood and firebrick

        red

such blood   beads of serpent
        purple
    beads and bells and teeth
            that shimmer blaze
        down
                frederick
                            street
throngs as thick as
        wet gravel

  super 8 red
        and burnt clay
    beards
        diffused and refracted
            into lime green
                        lamé   luminous
                eyelets in
                    mad bull
        masks
                    cadmium red or
                lilac palms
        a sceptre he holds
                nemo
        shone black against this
                glitter
    diamante and frivolous
        feathers
        glimmer
on his face
                    wet and
supple is his idiom
                sweat
and endless technicolor prayers
        o mother of pearl with
    scent of fresh paintwire bent

which emblems are these
                river gods with
such rampant plumages
        startling in
the firesky?

the moko jumbie
        12 foot up
                stilts of wood
        painted white/white
    painted wood
                slack
        bruised whip of hips that
        keep time
all these
                colours
            that drip from his face
                his apollic bust
        monoxylous
        to represent water
                    obatala or spiritual
                        baptist

                    the mud band stretched there
            from g to b flat
            on keate street
outside deluxe cinema
                waiting
for charlie's roots
                to pass
                so much tar get jam
        on that barbergreen
                so much blood spume
                    from them steel wheel
    of steel   band   pushing

                down from hilltop
                        rolling bass drum
                                across the dust and big yard stage

                we uses to run
        from oil and tar band
                long time
                                burrokeets
                        an dem jab mollasie
                        devil mas
        from casablanca badjohn
                and hell's yard catelli all-stars pan man
        from dr rat and renegades
                and all these wars
                that music make
        when two band clash

        through all these wars
                we carried
        our mother's basket
                plaited with italicised straw
                                for her rugged harvest
                        of red koolaid
        and baked chicken
                        thighs
                                elegiac
                pressed against
          poems in this nervous
                        centre
                pulled   she
                        our small hands
             and splinters
                        where the weight
                cut
                        her shoulder
                                to fragments

when a bottle smash
                and the band get slack
an scatter
        our laughter swung
 from deep magenta haze
                some wound there
        her breast still
                        sore still

these wires
        bent into purple tiaras
and guinea fisherman poles
        flags and their emblems
                which shook rome
of its silver
        with dread
                beards of mud
   from creation
                and dissonance of
                        mud
black benin topsoil
of earth
                moist word
        of the griot
come his come
chanting
        from some house of din
                we abseiled from
to find him
        in a dusty field
                stuttering
                in ray minor

— sans humanité—

                    charlotte street and duke street corner
simple so we suckin sugarcane
                    watching mas
but all this temporal till
        wednesday's ash
                    we there
        satyr-tailed
at green corner
        we was
        bullet hot by roxy roundabout
        we was
        chippin foot an shufflin
                    like paradiddle
rimshot
    like galvanise
                    from hurricane
        we there
at green corner
            when bottle pelt
                    and the road get red
            from all that
super 8
            saturates

        at ariapita avenue
 adam smith square
queens park west and cipriani boulevard
        where the asphalt blinks
                    with decals strewn from
sequined queens
        pixelated in
                    the st anns air
under the
    almond trees
at memorial square
        we were

112

flesh in the swelter of
                    tropic fruit
              soaked
                    brineways
              fire
        and the lash of it

        was a hummingbird
                    coast we sailed to
a masked ball
                    we inherited
masks we stole
                    mansions we overturned in
              rum we cooked with

                    so shallow is this
memory that it pierced me like
              chiricahuan arrowhead
                          cereous
drowned it in double
              beaten goatskin drums
from gust and plywood
              junctions
where bliss throat sparkles
there
              even
like sea silt and
                    jetty fish
near port authority where
                    cruise ships landed like
              spaceships to this
dreamscape

              contemplating
        the road

our
        verge of memory
                split like cane with
canboulay fire
        with gilpin
to planass // left marks from
                flat side of the blade
and my grandmother
        said how steelbands
                used to clash
                        there
in that sacred place
near belmont valley road
        so dark would never
            catch her
                in port of spain

        we saw the webbed wings of the carnival queen
                        isis fluttering
        in her second skin
                peep
her halo
        and the underlungs
                of her sadness
and the sequined spice of her
        perspiring
captured by blue box flash tube
        telefusion and diffuse relay
                these images
        the clack calacka clack of
                the midnight robbers
                collection box
                        and his tall black
        overcoat with stars and
                skulls and smoke
        black/skin

                    glistening white
                              with paint
and deep signal
                    red
                       fresh paint scent
sent along the avenues
    was when we knew
                    carnival was coming
so polaroid on this hot road
                          with tall
stems of the jumbie
        rode stilts to
                        cross   back
    over   oceans
                and over from
                    shack to stage
                perched on
        barbed wire
– spew and revolution –
        and the cosquelle and
                the dame lorraine
lifting her dress
        was saturnalia

we   carried him
                the king
collapsed upon
                our shoulders
    he wore wings
bent from mongoose bone
        headpiece of gold
                radiating
from persian goldmines
                road make to walk
so we carried him
                towards st james

in this blue devil leap
                nothing
        is sacred
                except his tunic of abstract
silk and mollusc

– muscle in the air –
        to abasia
                was miles
                we walked
                without knowing
and each street the next
        to saturate
        the bliss of it
opaque steep
with bougainvillea
        & super 8
        red

PETE KALU

OLD RADICALS

Hot with indignation
apartheid, Special Patrol and the NF
we nailed placards together, wrote speeches
flung each other over barricades
our hands on rocks and riot shields

We cried, hugged, slept, dreamed
made the 5am calls from cells
brothers for the Cause

Years intervened
the Anti Deportation Campaign calls came
your support phoned through
signature on the fifth page of the petition,
an approving onlooker to the march
at length your name appeared only on campaign chain emails
occasionally and then never

Me? I found myself worrying about fresh nappies
as we marched
grew content to listen to others' speeches
traded in the car that constantly broke down
found jackets and trousers easy to wear

That afternoon we met on Liverpool Street, fumbled
with the old handshakes
and as you pulled away again I glanced
back at a friendship cooled

JACKIE KAY

THE RED GRAVEYARD

There are some stones that open in the night like flowers
Down in the red graveyard where Bessie haunts her lovers.
There are stones that shake and weep in the heart of night
Down in the red graveyard where Bessie haunts her lovers.

Why do I remember the blues?
I am five or six or seven in the back garden;
the window is wide open;
her voice is slow motion through the heavy summer air.
Jelly roll. Kitchen man. Sausage roll. Frying pan.

Inside the house where I used to be myself,
her voice claims the rooms. In the best room even,
something has changed the shape of my silence.
Why do I remember her voice and not my own mother's?
Why do I remember the blues?

My mother's voice. What was it like?
A flat stone for skitting. An old rock.
Long long grass. Asphalt. Wind. Hail.
Cotton. Linen. Salt. Treacle.
I think it was a peach.
I heard it down the ribbed stone.

I am coming down the stairs in my father's house.
I am five or six or seven. There is fat thick wallpaper
I always caress, bumping flower into flower.
She is singing. (Did they play anyone else ever?)
My father's feet tap a shiny beat on the floor.

Christ, my father says, that some voice she's got.
I pick up the record cover. And now. This is slow motion.

118

My hand swoops, glides, swoops again.
I pick up the cover and my fingers are all over her face.
Her black face. Her magnificent black face.
That's some voice. His shoes dancing on the floor.

There are some stones that open in the night like flowers
Down in the red graveyard where Bessie haunts her lovers.
There are stones that shake and weep in the heart of night
Down in the red graveyard where Bessie haunts her lovers.

PRIDE

When I looked up, the black man was there,
staring into my face,
as if he had always been there,
as if he and I went a long way back.
He looked into the dark pool of my eyes
as the train slid out of Euston.
For a long time this went on
the stranger and I looking at each other,
a look that was like something being given
from one to the other.

My whole childhood, I'm quite sure,
passed before him, the worst things
I've ever done, the biggest lies I've ever told.
And he was a little boy on a red dust road.
He stared into the dark depth of me,
and then he spoke:
"Ibo," he said. "Ibo, definitely."
Our train rushed through the dark.
"You are an Ibo!" he said, thumping the table.
My coffee jumped and spilled.
Several sleeping people woke.
The night train boasted and whistled
through the English countryside,
past unwritten stops in the blackness.

"That nose is an Ibo nose.
Those teeth are Ibo teeth," the stranger said,
his voice getting louder and louder.
I had no doubt, from the way he said it,
that Ibo noses are the best noses in the world,
that Ibo teeth are perfect pearls.
People were walking down the trembling aisle
to come and take a look

as the night rain babbled against the window.
There was a moment when
my whole face changed into a map,
and the stranger on the train
located even the name
of my village in Nigeria
in the lower part of my jaw.

I told him what I'd heard was my father's name.
Okafor. He told me what it meant,
something stunning,
something so apt and astonishing.
Tell me, I asked the black man on the train
who was himself transforming,
at roughly the same speed as the train,
and could have been
at any stop, my brother, my father as a young man,
or any member of my large clan,
Tell me about the Ibos.

His face had a look
I've seen on a MacLachlan, a MacDonnell, a MacLeod,
the most startling thing, pride,
a quality of being certain.
Now that I know you are an Ibo, we will eat.
He produced a spicy meat patty,
ripping it into two.
Tell me about the Ibos.
"The Ibos are small in stature
Not tall like the Yoruba or Hausa.
The Ibos are clever, reliable,
dependable, faithful, true.
The Ibos should be running Nigeria.
There would be none of this corruption."

And what, I asked, are the Ibos' faults?
I smiled my newly acquired Ibo smile,
flashed my gleaming Ibo teeth.
The train grabbed at a bend,
"Faults? No faults. Not a single one."

"If you went back," he said brightening,
"The whole village would come out for you.
Massive celebrations. Definitely.
Definitely," he opened his arms wide.
"The eldest grandchild – fantastic welcome.
If the grandparents are alive."

I saw myself arriving
the hot dust, the red road,
the trees heavy with other fruits,
the bright things, the flowers.
I saw myself watching
the old people dance towards me
dressed up for me in happy prints.
And I found my feet.
I started to dance.
I danced a dance I never knew I knew.
Words and sounds fell out of my mouth like seeds.
I astonished myself.
My grandmother was like me exactly, only darker.

When I looked up, the black man had gone.
Only my own face startled me in the dark train window.

BUSH FIRE

That fire, they said, was red as red as red
as red as a fox, your lips, a cherry;
that fire, they said, spread and spread and spread,
faster than a cheetah or a nasty rumour;
that fire, they said, was hot, so hot, so hot,
hotter than lava or an African summer.

That fire, they said, was angry, very angry.
For three roaring days, it danced wildly, wildly, wildly.
Wild as flamenco, strip the willow, a Highland fling.
That fire, they said, had a big bad mouth,
swearing, spluttering, "Bring it on! Bring it on!"

That fire, they said, wolfed down the lot –
the lovely little homes, the trees, the land.
That fire, they said, left nothing behind at all:
one blackened trail, one sad scorched story.

RED RUNNING SHOES

I wore some other girl's red running shoes
with real spikes like rose thorns under my foot.

I got into position: my limbs seriously tense,
one knee on the asphalt, one foot flat, all that.

I crouched over, hands down, like a predator
ready for prey; and took off, took flight

on the red running track, so fast I could be fear
running, a live fright, a chance vision.

My dark hair wild in the wind.
My arms pounding light years, thin air, euphoria.

I flew past in some other girl's red running shoes,
round the red track near the railway line.

I raced straight towards the future.
The past was left standing behind, waving.

I ran and ran; my feet became the land.
I couldn't tell if the ground was moving under my feet,

shifting sand, or if I might ever just stop, like a heartbeat.
It felt as if I would run for ever, hard pounding feet,

until I ran right into myself, years on,
sat still, heavy, past forty, groaning, the streak lightning gone.

ALVIN KIRBY

HIGH HEELS

You look good now, but just you wait
till you're 53 and your veins
spring out like Stilton cheese

and you're suffering from arthritis.
Where's the sex appeal in this?

The trainers that you wear to work –
cumbersome comfort
for the sole compared to these.

At what point do you slip them on?
The main entrance? Or round the block
where you are surely out of sight

of all the people you must convince
that you're as confident as they think?

There's so much pressure, blisters grow –
you think the plaster doesn't show,

it's nothing like the tone of skin;
you're grimacing. You hobble in.

Sculptured bondage for the feet –
and in the western world you're free
to vote for what you want to wear;

Huh! No better than man's mannequins
in ready-to-please uniform.

Man's grand designs on woman again
while shuffling about in Birkenstocks –

Is this the equality you want
the choice of Prada or Patrick Cox?

The way they make you totter about –
your calves pull taut, your bum sticks out.

Try sprinting down a flight of steps
you'll sprain your ankle, break your neck.

Don't trip over man's chivalry –
the open doors and…

"Let me carry that for you,
you've got enough to think about",
like pimple-paving for the blind, and

how are you going to hold your pose
capsizing through steel grilles in those?

I'll lay my body on the ground
for you to walk all over me.

You're dressed to kill. I'll gladly die
a masochist's death
by stilettos 4 inches high.

You gratify this foul fetish –
Now if that's power, you got your wish.

Sad the day I became a size 10
and couldn't wear mum's red high heels again.

USHA KISHORE

THE SLAYING OF AUTUMN

Autumn
breathes her last
in cold air...

Her lover,
the sun,
wrestles with
the sword of
Orion –
a hapless
battle of
light and dark...

My dreams,
frozen by
arctic winds,
hibernate
under
pine trees;
they will
wake up
when autumn
is reborn
and dance
with the gold
of leaves...

Robin,
slayer of
autumn,
with blood
on her chest,

pecks at my
thoughts –
she is the
high priestess
at the altar of
Solstice…

JANET KOFI-TSEKPO

THE VISIT

I see you come to me with your head bowed.
Let me look, as any soldier of mine
would look at you – a sweet, fresh concubine
hauled in from the Red Sea. Don't tell me how
you really got here, I don't care. For now,
it's enough for us to sit and drink wine.
Come closer! Look at how those eyes shine
like ice. Your hands are cold blades on my brow;
and yet there's something in your face that burns
like a circle of fire in a lion's den,
making me feel a kind of loyalty
beyond kin. Every part of me yearns
for your heat. Sweet Judith, tell me again
why you visit my tent like royalty?

4

Beauty, to me, is about being comfortable in your own skin. That, or a kick-ass red lipstick.
Gwyneth Paltrow

Be on the alert, like the red ant that moves with its claws wide open.
Ugandan Proverb

When the time came for her to give birth, there were twin boys in her womb. The first to come out was red, and his whole body was like a hairy garment...
Genesis 25:24-34

KOKUMO

REDLIGHT!

ebre weh dat mi guh
a just redlight
mi try hard fi find a likkle job
a just redlight
nuh care wha qualification mi hab
a just redlight
mi tek a walk out a street
a just redlight
fi try find food fi eat
a just redlight
de situation out fi dribe mi mad
a just redlight
a mussi pocket dem whau mi grab
a just redlight
it red! it red! it redda dan… red
it dread! it dread! it dreada dan… dread!
it red! it red! it redda dan… red
ebre weh dat mi guh
a just redlight
mi put foot ina supa-markit
a just redlight
but de sing ting dem dare nuh raatid
a just redlight
police ina radio car
a just redlight
dem dou care who yuh are
a just redlight
it red! it red! it redda dan… red
it dread! it dread! it dreada dan… dread!
it red! it red! it redda dan… red
ebre weh dat mi guh
a just redlight

mi dress up ina suit an tie
a just redlight
nuh care how hard mi try
a just redlight
dem still cyaan tell mi why
a just redlight
instead dem a tell pay lie
a just redlight
it red! it red! it redda dan… red
it dread! it dread! it dreada dan… dread!
it red! it red! it redda dan… red!

VASUNDHARA KULKARNI

RED DIAMONDS

Lambada woman at work
swiftly shifts
brick-stacked iron trays
then lifts
a cement–filled platter
to place it
over a coiled cushion
on her head.

Even as her back
bares itself
like the summer's earth,
mirrors
on her bright red attire
dazzle
in the noonday glare.

In a tiny space half-shaded
by the fine sand
and the hard granites,
a lady suckles her young
in the canopy of her sari.
As she pauses

and looks up to drink water,
her eyes almost close;
yet
the vermillion on her forehead
is sun herself.

In a distant desert,
as women dressed

in the hues of an unhurried dusk
prepare to grind spice
by a carpet of hot peppers,

they blaze
like strokes of saffron and scarlet
on a camel-coloured canvas;

even with soaked armpits
and parched skins
they flicker

like red diamonds

shot forth
by volcanoes of fathomless force
and strengthened

in the bosom of energies
unbound, unknown.

ROI KWABENA

SURE, REDS

so it is – if yuh aint red
yuh considered dead

me fadder say is victory an' strength
like we flag unfurled;
ah hear from young: red woman badd
so only eat Julie mango if it red

orisha flag red
red as akoko blood fuh sacrificed libation

kalenda man bois tie wid red cloth tuh
fuh de spirits to bust nuff head
jamette does also dress up in red
to giddy man head more dan babash

spiritual baptist mudder red headtie prophesy
ringing bells on de corner

black power red
vast demonstrating power tuh de people
soldiers mutiny an' de hills ran red
wen coast guard guns bombarded
til' false amnesty teken fuh granted

as ah Muslim in Trinidad
yuh won't be caught dead wearin' red
except on Hosay midnight
as a flag-bearing Shiite
or fasting devotee dancing ah heavy red sun
buh some extremist consider red sinful…
djab colour full ah sexual passions
like bacchnal, red for jouvert in de blistering early sun

angry protesters marched around de embassy in red jersey
"Hands off Grenada! Hands of Cuba!"
til' sadly… leadership crisis reared ah ugly head
proletariat blood flowed red in de streets from Fort Rupert
as Maurice like a moor now bishop violently deposed
plus USA wid self-appointed red acolytes invaded
dat bloody sad October month in Grenada
was really hot! red hot in dem days
communist… PRG member or Rasta Socialist Marxist Leninist
hunted from door tuh door

soon to red house parliament was invaded for ah coup
an' dis time de streets ah Port of Spain flowed red wid blood
like wen Ineri rub down wid roucou
tuh massacre umpteen español in sangre grande
or wen nuff rioters pelt big stone
at ah stained glass tuh honour Columbus statue
inna de same red house
fuh Governor Moloney tun red in anger

buh now wen is Hindu Holi time
in mount gay abandon we wood be awash in abeer
singing parang fuh christmas in red
or holier dan thou follow katholic procession
in a red fuh la divina pastora

den came de real football fever days
all de way from Port of Spain tuh Nuremburg
fuh de world cup
oui boys in red: soca warriors
de place was awash in red
over a million painted up in red
till de English man pull out oui player in red locks
we lose de game
red wid disappointment
so we wine widout cryin' an' paint the town red

2007-elections 'round de corner
politricks in red
oui red again
PNM in red supporters vowing victory before voting
while CoP split from UNC shouting
dem rally go be de real RED

see Reds, sometimes ah does see red
knowin' me patrimony siphoned abroad
in ah rich hydrocarbon-producin' country
before it red in de sky foreday morn
many still have tuh watchman standpipe fuh water

if yuh aint red?

"it may not last as long as the red house fire"

JUDITH LAL

RED, AS RED AS YOU LIKE

Sameer Shah the dashing young
dentist and natural stand-in for the
wayward hero who goes down with a bout
of something, takes one look at my tooth
as though looking at *Chomolungma*
pushing her wisdom up between India
and China and says, *Your name, it means*
red. Open a little wider please. In response
I cannot help but bite the mirror. The
Victorians thought it was always a healthy
colour to have next to skin. I imagine
the women waving off husbands who get
smaller and ever smaller in tweed and
singlets until disappearing up into white out,
into the lamasery of the snows, while they
stay home in underwear that contrary to
popular belief was red, as red as you like.

SUNDRA LAWRENCE

PLAY

After you come
the sun relaxes

a tiny pinkish glow
develops in the horizon.

You say that late afternoon
is scotch, slow and golden,

opening to the heavens.
I hope we can do this again tomorrow.

ARRIVAL

Paprika saris mind pots of rice and rassam,
clean white towels are readied
as a town camps on veranda steps
talks through sleep, awaits your arrival.

You are born with Jafna soil hair
torn cinnamon bark; its red reaches
every mud-hutted home in the village.
You arrive in the middle of night's time.

Babies born at midnight grow up unafraid,
your Cinamma would say, made you talk louder
march barefoot, bold in the backyard;
small footprints engrave the broken soil;
not one of your seven siblings followed.

After school you listen to Amma's stories,
watch starch fill water and spill
over her wrists as she washes rice,
you find a rusty pan to catch rain;
it leaks like pomegranate seeds on tin.

Married now, you pack for your migration
a case of cotton clothes,
rosary between your fingers and thumb;
dressed in a mango flesh sari
you wonder what colour the sky will be
when you get there.

SEGUN LEE-FRENCH

BREATHING PALM OIL

You would be a sack
pressed against the timber
of a tea clipper,
a stowaway memory

a bite of pregnant
air, beside a *suya* joint,
a beggar's stolen meal

a splash of sauce
on stiff brocade, uninvited
wedding guest that stays

a plastic bottle emptied & refilled till it cracks,
leaking its soul, red earth
onto the road

a teasing smile suggesting
it could be bartered, a promise
of salty lips

a *nyash* whose perfect curves
touch
the centre of the palm,

forever moist.

DAWN LIBURD

SCHOOL RUN

Earth's core.
Magma
spews.
Cars, trucks, vans,
a throbbing river
of lava,
dammed
by a red light.
The warming sky
stews
clouds, dripping
palm oil
on knuckles
that manoeuvre
pushchairs
to school gates,
where scarlet blazers
cluster
plucking conkers
from a gutter
of rusting leaves.

JOHN LYONS

SUGAR CANE BUNDOWN

His cries were raw vermillion.
He was left in Tropic of Cancer heat
chained with his agony to a calabash tree.
He saw behind closed eyelids
the hot colour of his blood, pulsing.

When he opened his eyes, he saw
a lacerated sky of darkening clouds
was haemorrhaging flocks of scarlet ibis;
and he remembered the faces in the night,
red and shadow-black like animated masks
lit by the fire of burning sugarcane.

He knew then
that tomorrow
and tomorrow
and tomorrow
Massa's bullpistle would be wild
with the lust for blood
glistening on black skin.

BUG OF THE PRICKLY PEARS

The Aztecs treasured it
as they did their palaces of gold.

It is Pliny's tale of cinnabar:
the dragon and the elephant
mixing their blood in mortal combat.

It is the symbolic colour-pledge
of cardinals to die for their faith;
the Crusaders' cross.

It was the bright tunic
of Cromwell's New Model Army.

Turner's sky colour
for his masterpiece *Slave Ship*.

It is seduction on the lips of courtesans;
the cochineal's legacy
to the Flanders poppy.

SHEREE MACK

TIMES IN RED

i. Evening

Across the river in a red brick Tyneside flat,
cramped and dark, all velvet cushions and figurines,
is a couple. It isn't their home. They are playing house.
He is strolling through the hanging beads,
carrying a thick crust pepperoni pizza with extra salami.
She is chopping tomatoes, lettuce and cucumber, quickly.
Under the window, they sit, across the pull-out table.
He lights a candle and takes her hand, smiles.
She looks out over slated roofs to see the sun go down.
They eat in silence, chewing the food slowly.
The cheese is stringy and the pepperoni is spicy.
The lettuce is crisp and the tomatoes are juicy.
They talk into the night with kisses and cuddles.
She looks out beyond his face to the moon.

ii. Morning

Dear Tom

Between the rows of brick houses, I was walking
and thought of you. Snatches of words came my way,
said you were with someone else. But your look was severe.
What would have been if we had stayed together?
You were grounded. I was always looking around
that corner for something besides.
God knows, you had your work cut out for you with me.
I hope the women who followed haven't suffered, much.
Call it a guilty conscience, if you like, whatever.
I'm in a good place and wish the same for you.

Maybe I didn't like the way things ended.
Maybe I could have given you the truth.
I was all redwebbed eyeballs from romance fiction.
I didn't know the love you were giving.

Keep well, thinking of you, sometimes.

Gillian

iii. Afternoon

Dear Tom

It has rained and rained since the letter left me to you.
Can't we be adult about this? I've changed.
Did you become a social worker?
Your brother's wedding, did she wear scarlet?
Remember, when you used to sneak into his room
to find "evidence"? Pills and condoms and we joined the dots.
We banged our hips off each other, waiting for a better time,
the best time, more excuses.
University came, and so did other people.
You still came to me and shared my bed
for your first time, mine too, you thought.
But what hurt me, as you lay naked afterwards,
was the wintriness of your words: the child,
still scared in the disguise of a man.

Keep well, thinking of you, sometimes.

Gillian

iv. Dawn

Dear Gillian

I tried to forget you like the dead, but
the impact of your letter is such that I almost see you;
your distant eyes and your tangled auburn hair.
When your date fell through, or you needed money
or when your sister died, I was there
but I still wasn't enough for you. I feel shame.
I wouldn't say "used" as that's too common a word,
manipulated is more fitting.
With this letter, I hope to stop all other letters.
We're two different people now and
I realise, we were two different people then.
I wish you luck. No I don't. I wish you nothing.
Please let me get on with my life.
That was your goal. Let it be mine.

Tom

SKIN DEEP

I below the window, working the roses.
Little bugs eat the roses,
some leaves had fallen off
so I chewing tobacco leaves
to spit on the roses.
It kills the bugs and almost kills me.
I heaving in mi guts with the chewing.
I can't see how the men can favour it.
To me, it's bitter and ugly.
It looks like I spitting out slugs.

I below the window, when I hear the Missus:
"I swear, if Clem doesn't stop buying Negroes,
there'll be no money left for dresses."
I holding in mi laugh
and crouching further down,
as the Missus could have
a whole heap of dresses – silks and satins
and still be no beauty.
Beauty is only dress deep with that woman.
She be a stick and ridged with it.

Missus says, "He gone bought
another Negro. We not made of money."
There's two ways to bring them in – good or bad.
Massa walk him in bad.
Massa setting up on his seat
pistol in his belt, like he something big.
He's walking naked, alone, in front of the horse,
neck shackled, with rope to the saddle.
Every time the horse stop
he is pulled up, neck jerked.

They stop in front of the quarters
and I getting a look at his back.
The skin criss-cross like Missus stitching,
raised like my hand, but muscles still strong.
I red like hibiscus tea
and all them around me brown.
So I blinking, as he is black,
as black as the night, as black as the marble
outside the front of the Big House,
dust clinging to his sweat.

His head is high like the sun.
His head is as high as an eagle.

HAZEL MALCOLM

RED FLAG

Blood of angry workers
surrendered to the middle ground
reborn out of the wounds of the voiceless
on the streets of distress
on the streets of possibility
may you rise up once more, and
fly

BLUES IN THE BLACK COUNTRY

In the heat and the sweat and the blackness
Swirling shades of ebony embroil together in the ruby shadows
Smelting fragments of molten desire
Slag oozes from the dandy and infuses
With the sweet orange blossom and ginger
Embers of gilded women line the wall
Red ribbon glares rave across the room
The track fades
Only cinders of the moment remain
In the heat and the sweat and the blackness.

JACK MAPANJE

RETINAL SCREENING, CHRISTMAS 2006

Anyone arrived for retinal screening?
Hands up. She picks her client like
A school teacher. Sits him on straight
Chair. Close left eye with left hand.
Which line can you read from my eye
Testing board? Tick. Now right eye
With right hand. You can read each
Letter in the last line? That must be
The eye we removed the cataract last
Time. So when Christmas comes she
Must monitor whatever grey his eyes
Have gathered. And hand out tissue
Hankies for her eye drop installation.
The trick, she finds, is to close eyes
After drops. And they'll fizz, sharp
At first, then warm – the drops that
Swell pupils before photographing
Inside the eye – the bit that's irksome.
Phase two. Sit in the waiting room
Before the photographer's reckoning,
Where the Christmas tree menaces
Yours at home whose evergreen apex
Star glints, branches draped in red,
Gold, silver chains, bells, balls glisten.
Then the dark room. Place chin on
Little scoop of camera's stand. Lock
Left eye into camera. Do you see
The red line? Flash! Eye burns? Blurs?
It would, wouldn't it, first white blur,
Then blue, then white again. Right
Eye next, all the while concentrating
On the red line. Flash! Three blurs?

Done. Don't drive home yet; recover
Full sight in car park, where at least
A hundred aeroplanes and Christmases
Are fogged out, you hear, which won't
Signify, as you marvel at the number
Of rituals that multiply each year.

VALERIE MASON-JOHN

PLAYING DEAD

Curled up in my mother's bed
Tight like a screw. Back to back
I can't sleep. I'm playing dead.
I simulate sleep. Avoid her smacks.
Wander off to somewhere snug.
Soft warm fingers approach my spine.

I roll over. Hoping for a hug.
It's hard playing dead. I feel divine.
Fingers stroke my new-formed breasts.
She spreads my legs. I wet the bed.
I am aroused, flushed red, unable to rest.
But I'm still playing dead.

She abandons me for a Marlborough Light.
I'm still aching for tomorrow night.

KAREN McCARTHY

ROUTEMASTER

I cannot catch this last red bus,
or hear the last bell ding ding!
It's not what I want, but I must.

Why didn't we kick up more of a fuss?
Write to the council – petition the King.
I cannot catch this last red bus,

if I do, I'll forget the two of us,
completed like yang and yin.
It's not what I want, but I must.

Then, nothing lay between us but trust,
love bound us together like string.
I cannot catch this last red bus.

Remember: life's as fair as it's just,
and barely as long as a fling.
It's not what I want, but I must.

My mittenless self could never have guessed
the sorrow our journey might bring.
I cannot catch this last red bus.
It's not what I want, but I must.

THE WORSHIPFUL COMPANY OF POMEGRANATE SLICERS

Before you know this apple of many seeds,
this globe of islands and seasons and blood,
it does not matter whether your knife
is serrated. All that matters is the cut, the spill,
a taste so sour only salt can make it sweet.
At its heart revealed: a glistening star.

Punica granatum you are the hidden star
of David: six hundred and thirteen seeds
in the white of the aril, each one a sweet
boiled red by a meticulous God whose blood
seeps blue on sands where Bedouins spill
stories like goat guts from the tip of a knife.

Orion went hunting with his dog and his knife.
He carved Side's sun-skinned city as his star.
She shone so bright Queen Hera vowed to spill
her calyx crown and scatter her limbs like seeds.
Goddesses! You've never seen such a blood-
thirsty lot; a rival's head tastes sweet.

Gods are no better. When Hades lured sweet
Persephone deep underground, no knife
was needed: just a contract signed in blood,
a tempting daffodil and the garnet star,
his jewel of winter. She ate six seeds,
then let all she ever dared desire spill

on to her tongue; let pink, sharp juice spill
over lips stained purple with sweet, sweet
abandon. But before too long bitter seeds
of doubt began to grow and Hades' knife
was a smile that eclipsed her guiding star.
Demeter: her light, her source, her blood.

Come inside! Wet your head in the blood
of the fruit, let the exhilaration of wine spill
into your throat. Breathe in, inhale the star
dust. Pull the pin, explode every sweet
secret, watch each one blaze across a knife-
slashed sky. Soft earth will catch the seeds.

Slice the circle while your blood runs sweet.
All you will spill with your sickle knife
is a star from a cluster of seeds.

RICHARD "RICH BLK" MKOLOMA

COLOUR BLIND

i didn't think
i
ever
understood her
crimson.
i tasted shiraz
while she fed me
merlot tinged with swollen bluffs
i misread as hearts
she kept hers
close to chest
played diamonds
to suit my bloodshot moods
& wore spectacles rose-tinted and precise
matching move for mood
replacing bruises for a sanguine
disposition
i misread as
happy,
rosy even.
funny,

i never imagined myself colour blind
yet i mixed her blues for blushes
& became ultraviolet
not realising i only fed her inflamed purple raisins
scolded skin and caused history tarnished.
suntans are meant to be earned.
her crimson deserved urgency
danger
approached with alarming relish
and zeal matched only by
vermillion dawns illuminating the lady in scarlet dressed

to kill
trepidation.
she didn't
want lukewarm.

volcanic eruptions,
slow kisses
soaked in waves of muted fury & constant –
she doesn't want lukewarm,

only red.

as seen through the eyes of a bull when target acquired
a tunnelled vision of eternal madness
a fever quenched only when nimble footed matador
is lanced & pain-stricken
knows they are living
witness to
lava.
haemorrhage.
& life.
flowing from battle scars
proudly adorned
&
i still don't know if she was
merlot
shiraz
or
just plain old red.

RAMAN MUNDAIR

LATE

Lateness worries you.
                The fear
of future. You
are never ready.

I stroke my belly, feel
reckless, open, waiting
while you check
the calendar again.

You want for sleep,
I practice lullabies,
round off afternoons with naps,
dreamplan nests for two.

Opening every window and door,
voice lifted, I tell you to go.
But you stay, small, hard.
closed. All night your knees

press against my back.
In the morning I leave you
blood red flowers pressed
onto white sheets.

LIFE DRAWING

Funked up sweet with sweat, paint
across your brow. You dance at
the canvas – you are feeling
creative tonight. Bach lifts the night air
and I am dizzy kissing your mouth rich
with dark, bitter chocolate. Your tongue
skimming the sky with stars while I
make secret magic. Fallopian flowers
that waft spheres into bloodspace.
Another cycle begins and the sacred
orbit takes place. We make an aria
out of breath. Cup the music to our ears,
listen and let the rhythm make its way,
listen and let the rhythm make its way.
Full with love and life,
our bodies draw a new picture.

KALI DAYS

Some days there is a tightness
in the air. A poverty of space
that claws and my foreign body

dreams of the welcoming mouth
of rapid rivers and the primed teeth
of mountain sides – the fall and the flow.

Some days the sound of traffic
draws you to dance in dual carriageways.
Flashing lights and the blare of horns

egg you on – fearless; Goddess Kali
you take on the dull red that blurs sense
and the little fists that beat

at the small of your back. Sharp,
bloated, aching – you
do not recognise yourself in this

wild place. Blood flowers
between your legs, bloodstones
on your tongue and blood lust

imprints the day and stains it red.
Exhausted you surrender to the moon
and let the transformation begin.

5

Out of the ash
I rise with my red hair
And eat men like air

Sylvia Plath

Red, red wine
Go to my head
Make me forget that I
Still need her so

Neil Diamond

SIMON M. MURRAY

SAVED BY SHOPPING

Inspired by and dedicated to (PRODUCT) RED™:
"…*the coming together of the distinct worlds of Africa and consumer-ism… The Ideals of celebration and empowerment* [which] *doesn't rely on negative images or guilt-driven participation… [and] …the joy that bringing two such tangibly different worlds together can create.*" (www.joinred.com)

dear santa
i would really like an afrikan baby
like brad and anjelina has
and maddonna
but just for weekends
as im still at school
a boy would be best and i like the fat bellys
but no flys please
if you dont have any left
then an i pod would be ok with tv and films on it
and this would be good to buy me becos
if you get a red one which is my favorit color
bono from u2 and gizell who is ~~gore gorg~~ gorjus
will stop afrikan aids
wich is really bad
you could also get me a red apple ipod nanno with camera and video on it
and other stuff too like a armarni watch converse sneakers and gap tee shirts
but i wouldnt be allowd the red american express card until im older
i have been good this year
and ive started to eat brocerley
and i bought two white braselets to make poverty history
love from
Simon xxx

LOVE FOR LABOUR LOST

I picked you
the best of the bunch
aroma of a new dawn
things could only get better

The prick of a thorn

I awake from slumber
vision clears
I see you for what you are:
plastic painted petals
barbed wire branches
serrated silicon leaves
swastika stem

bar code in black and white
brand name fluorescent
manufactured in Asia, the "Middle East", Latin America, Afrika…
made in Rome, Britain, Europe, USA

I fight for breath
your sweet smell sickens
synthetic cyanide stink
choking chemical perfume
Venus flytrap by nature
a rose by PR-focus group name
beauty in the eye of the contract holder

vampire rose
roots tunnelled in foreign lands
rivers of blood to colour your bulbous head

I will not pick you again.

DALJIT NAGRA

THE BREAKDOWN

That human by the brook – how they probe
if it's a Blue Skin or a Brown Skin
or it's prognosed
as a White Skin or a Black Skin
but if it's a 50/50 then it's diatribed
as Mixed Race!
That's how needle-toting
are the Brown and the Blue Brood across
the drowning earth with their bloodthirsty eyes
for every shade in its place!
They'd stormtrooper to bash
the labs that are hunting to bear out
the everyman percentiles
of that human-by-the-brook's dawn-of-time-to-the-now
D   N   A

GRACE NICHOLS

ICONS

Everything foreign was better than local
or so it seemed when I was a child
but perhaps the grown-ups lied –
the shimmering lie
of the emperor's new clothes.

Among the English icons praised to the skies –
iceapples, Yardleys, grapes,
the unseen snowflake.
We'd watch the shopkeeper's crafty hands
among the apple-crates.

The way he'd carefully
pull back the crinkled tissue
as if it was cotton-wool
and the glistening red unbittens
jewels instead of fruit.

On Christmas morning if we were lucky
we'd delve deep to find an apple ruby,
our stocking's only bit of edible magic.
Who knows why I was hardly tempted
to bite or ravish?

Even now in England's supermarkets
I instinctively leave the polished red –
a wary Snow White going instead
for the common locals –
Cox's orange-pippins, russetts.

Still I must say that it gladdens the heart
to see how both my apple-eating daughters
have emerged; carefully avoiding the pith and pips,
while drooling endlessly over the mango
two sun-starved Eves –

making a meal of the old creation myth.

MAFU NQOBILE

I WANT

Yah! Let me tell you,
let me tell you about the struggle.
In 2000, thousands of people lay dead.
The streets were red with blood.

I want to tell you about how people suffered.
Some spent seven days without anything to eat.
Some were forced to walk hundreds of miles.
People were struggling,
people were crying,
I want to tell you how people were disappearing.

Brothers and fathers were forced to join the ruling party.
Youngsters were forced to join the Green Bomber, youth militia.
Mothers and sisters were raped,
Some were brutally raped in front of their husbands,
in front of their children.
I was scared, very scared.
My tears were running down my cheeks
when I saw a young girl raped in front of me
She was raped by four strong men, *isiqwabalanda*.

I sweated! Sweated, shivering, could find nothing to say,
I could only shake my head; my hands were holding my mouth.

Let me tell you about the bloodshed.
I want to tell you about the white farmers
who were forced to leave their farms;
they left their properties, not allowed to carry anything away.
Let me tell you, and I want to tell you,
some were beaten,
their farms burned to ashes,
crops were slashed by the so-called war veterans.

I want to tell you about how people were murdered,
some were found with body parts missing.
I was breathing heavily, heavily
when my friend was hanged on a mango tree.
Nqobani was innocent, Nqobani was a kind man,
but he died because he was an enemy to the ruling party.
He died whilst fighting for change.
When he was found, his private parts were missing.
I say to you, Nqobani, rest in peace.
Tears can dry but memories can't die.
I will always remember you.
I will keep on fighting until we are set free.

I want to tell you about this government,
this government that has totally destroyed
our beloved country.
From His Excellency the President to his Excellency the Dictator,
our Chief Commander is now the Thief Commander,
and the doctors are the dealers.
Let me tell you, and I will tell you what I want.

All the government knows is how to maintain its soldiers
and policeman by buying them new boots, new uniforms,
new underpants and new baton sticks,
while the economy is going down, down!
Things are hard to get:
no ballpoint, no sugar, no fuel, no water –
even toilet paper you can't find.
O cry beloved country, o cry beloved country.

I want to tell you everything, and I will tell you,
from south to north, east to west.
From kwaBulawayo to Harare via Gweru,
all corners of the country.
Let me tell you, let me tell you.
I want to tell you.

TOLU OGUNLESI

THE TROPHY

I

Has red ever won a trophy,
Eternal contender on the long-
List of ancient rainbows?

II

The lives in a London blast:
Different dreams strung through
With a common death,
Served up to fate
In the same rich redness.

In the same rich redness
Bethlehem blossoms.
In the narrow streets,
Where Pharisees once smelled adulterers out, is
A masked gunman playing hide-and-seek.

A masked gunman playing hide-and-seek
Is like a referee who keeps a red card up for
Ninety minutes. Does the human body now come
With small-print: "Liquid Contents Only"? When
Will red claim the biggest trophy of all?

Will red claim the biggest trophy of all
Now that the cities are crowned with tongues
Of fire (Amman, Baghdad, Bali,
London, Madrid, New York, Next), and
The children's cartridges are crammed with cherries?

The children's cartridges are crammed with cherries –
Plastic pretending to mount the Thrones of Lead.
Meanwhile, in other news: A blue planet is arrested,
And handcuffed with bright red ribbons, as
Blood breaks its covenants…

Blood breaks its covenant
With a young woman: *Do not pass GO,*
Do not stop seeing the red
Moon that rises between the thighs.
What shall she do to stop seeing red?

What shall she do to stop seeing red,
This earth, this womb
Of concrete, steel, sap and water,
Perched on the blind cusp of eternity.
Seconds away from eclipsing the real Red planet?

NII AYIKWEI PARKES

E BE SO
(Red, Accra, 1980)

"We have come to the cross-roads
And I must either leave or come with you." – Kwesi Brew ("The Mesh")

E be so we dey do am for here. He digs
a knife-wide hole in the ground
and looks up at me, his eyes like two worlds
colliding. I stand two feet back trying to conjure
the streets of London, holding onto
my six-year-old nonchalance in the face of death.

I hear say pipol for abroad dey shock them
plus lactric, but for here e be so we dey
do am. The chickens stop squawking
the moment Red squats, watching from a distance
as he prepares to cull their number. *Make you*
close your eyes. I do, but he pulls me forward
to see the white bird shut its eyes obediently
as he steps on its feet and wings.

You see, de hole be where de blood go go
e be for the pipol for de other side. You
for no kill chicken by heart, you hear? He wipes
the blade on the feathers, slits the neck
quickly, then holds the twitching body
over the hole until it stills, empty of fight.

After only nine months living in Accra, this is
initiation. Red is my living guide, my mystic.
I stare at the black hole beneath my feet,
still warm with blood, then at the eight
chickens lined up like fresh gladiators,

beginning to scratch the soil for prey, then
I hear him say: *Next time e be you go kill am,*
e be so we dey do am for here.

STRIPPING YAM

There was always us; two boys staking out
the kitchen as territory to invade;
new smells of the land born into us, a magnet

to the warm centre that made us
dark. We discovered a new vocabulary for hunger;
abele ni a sha̱, karklo, kelewele

and yɛlɛ ni a sha̱, yɛlɛ kɛ kontomire, yɛlɛ ni a shi̱
always yɛlɛ. We fell in love
with yam in its different guises, always beguiling.

We fell in love without knowing
its history, appreciating its journey from village
farm to town compound, without

reaching into the breast of the earth to feel it swell
from chunk to tuber; we were
enamoured without the encircling of yam's green

vines begging for attention, ours
was a love divorced from the past, a love inspired
by the dark, tough skin we knew

held fibre that could render us silent so our jaws
could move. Yɛlɛ, a name that
reconfigured our nervous systems, linked our ears

so intimately to our tongues
that the sound of frying yams made our hunger blues
switch to wet, red-pink

like litmus; we were so rooted to present joys till
1983 brought dry Sahel winds
and turned the word yele to whispers – *yɛlɛ, yɛlɛ*

so difficult to find, so tough
to conjure when the soil's fertility was compromised
and there was us, two boys

learning to live on a meal-a-day and the memory
of the sound of frying yams.
We became like yams; hard and dark as mango

tree bark in the relentless sun
smiling at each other, remembering past Aprils
when kindred birthdays gave

license to our family to cook and mash yams. Ot<u>o</u>
made by communal effort. Us
two boys cutting and stripping the yams of darkness

our mother washing the slices
and putting them in the pot till they emerged soft
to be mashed by our father then

mixed with spiced palm oil until a red mountain
topped with eggs; boiled, shelled
white declared that we were a year older, there

was always us; two boys sitting
around a plate, eating, dreaming, talking, growing
suffering together. And, like yams

the harder we are beaten, the stronger we bond; stick
to our purpose as fufu does
to fingers, so there is always us, two boys becoming

men. So each time I buy yams
their stripping becomes the telling of the story
of us, two boys, two men

hiding the fibre beneath our skins with smiles
and the sizzling sound of frying
yams is always ours; the sound of sweet struggle.

RED STRING

Sister Joy is celebrating
Jesus in a G-String.

Hollas, whoops and hallelujahs.
Dancehall makes way for divinity.

They're singing real loud
like a favourite Mary J tune;

praying for the sins
they've yet to commit.

They're bringing all they've got,
voices falling

as they sway in time,
arms flailing,

she eyes a "too high" heel,
a skin design peeping from a chest:

where his word is tattooed
on their hearts.

Her eyes shut, fingers crossed, legs closed,
oblivious to the ladder of her own fishnets,

she fingers the red string of her bible,
marks a psalm before snapping it shut.

Then she's singing again, real loud
and he's smiling, saying come as you are,

to the fisher of men
who makes fish clean.

MONIKA-AKILA RICHARDS

RED SAVIOUR

She is nine years old and worships red

shoes, hot air, autumn leaves
toys, angel wings, sunsets
buttons, dreams and clothes.

The smell of flowers
sends pulsating signals
stops the stench of death.

Wrapping her shawl tight
around her right stump,
pain instantly disappears.

Since she arrived
alone at the airport
red became her.

Camouflaging the scars
under her skin
inside out,

red makes everything real.

IONIE RICHARDS

THE LAST STAND

The Red House is silent now
I call but you do not hear
Concrete rises on a slope surveying Sulaymaniyah
Faded pink pockmarked paint
Peels against crimson hot sun

The Red House is silent now
I weep but you do not comfort
But it won't erase that day I left you alone
I said goodbye knowing
I would not be coming home
A surge of anger, rage, alarm, fear, shock
Unleashed revenge, rockets, rifles, terror and attack

The Red House is silent now
I hurt but you cannot feel
But it won't erase the memory
My blood mingles on splattered walls
Merging the red with the pain of loss

The Red House is silent now
I am free but you still mourn for me
But it won't bring back the dead
Rich and fertile grounds undulate
Pushing lilac and lilies from grassy mounds
In this crowded place I now rest
Silenced and bound

The Red House is silent now
I forgive but never forget
The decaying shell still reeks of death,
Kerosene mingles with acrid flesh

184

The Red House is silent now
I swirl in the breeze
As a Sunni flag ripples on the deserted roof
Devoid of mortars, rockets and Kalashnikovs
Under the hot sun concrete rises on a slope surveying Sulaymaniyah
In defiance
In memory
In silence.

THE SWEET TRAIL

Market vendors, inquisitive children
press into my space.
The terracotta midday sun burns.
"Buy sweets! Buy sweets!"
We oblige, oblivious to the journey.

We ride through sleepy villages
awakened at the sound of our coming.
Shouts of "Sweets!"
announce our arrival.

Hysterical shrill of small voices
comes on a wave of stampeding feet
hitting the red ochre Gambian earth.

Sweets scatter like seeds to grow
Western taste, tooth decay and poor diet,
chew sticks abandoned,
instruments of learning forgotten.
Instant gratification brings a chill;
the desperate chase begins.

Candy hits the dirt road
knowing we will reap what we sow.

ROGER ROBINSON

THE HUMAN CANVAS
For Mark Rothko

It's daylight seeping through your eyelids,
and you're stuck, and you want to get up.
It's blood, it's fire, the soft edge of a nightmare.

It's a gaping wound, the gut stink of a battlefield,
it's sacred malice, a slasher movie still,
it's daylight seeping through your eyelids.

It's a raw throat, a shout, the tip of the tongue.
A blood stain seeping through white sheets,
it's a gaping wound, the gut stink of a battlefield.

It's a canvas of skin peeled back
to coursing capillaries and chunks of fat.
It's a raw throat, a shout, the tip of the tongue.

It's a dark sienna of head and heart.
The cerise of a birthing womb.
It's a canvas of skin peeled back.

It's a coffin's red velvet lining,
a slashed artery gushing like an oil well.
It's a dark sienna of head and heart

down a chute of memory.
It's something that you forgot.
Deep, in your DNA, a final thought.

All that remains is the taste,
a metallic taste, filling your mouth,
down a chute of memory.

JOY RUSSELL

THE DUCHESS, THE CHERRIES, AND I

In my century, at my outdoor
swimming pool, decked on chaise longue,
is the Duchess of Queensbury
eating cherries from a crystal bowl.

This is my wet hallucination.

Gorging sweet ruby after ruby,
the Duchess fans herself.
In my mind, for a contemporary
look, I make her blond, bottled
like Marilyn, the dark roots
showing through.

I stand by the pool side,
next to tropical towel, apply
sun protection, Factor 15,
put on sunglasses like Jackie O,
dip my foot in – to create
a muscle, a ripple – blue
rectangle, otherwise, silent.

In her mouth disappears
the tiny polished globe:
stem, flesh, pit, then spit.
I feel her watching, not
taking me in – it goes like that
in history. Now, here, blue
marble, chlorine whiff.

Choked to death on cherries.

– mirage, silence, small ripple.

6

Just 'cause the dress is red satin don't mean
it'll come off easy!

Mae West

Red sky at night, shepherd's delight;
Red sky in the morning, shepherd's warning

Red hat, no knickers

JACOB SAM-LA ROSE

FLUSH

Instant rouge of a flushed cheek,
the echo of a branding clap, flaming
under the skin. We slow down, guilty
of trying to catch scraps of narrative

as we pass, arm in arm. She turns
and strides, hard, down the street
and into the early evening. Later,
we'll turn this over, wonder what

he's forgotten or said, what promise
failed, what sin she's judged him guilty of.
I'll remember her heels' staccato
on the pavement, the way her thighs

churn, mashing her full weight into
each step; how he stands, eyes
stunned like zeroes or dashes
on a reset clock display.

You'll note his solid chin, the bloom
across his face; his hand, its back
pressed against his mouth as if trying
to stop something from falling.

DEFINITION

If it were a smell? Pure heat
rising from a heaving room, packed

wall-to-wall, riding each surge and swell
of bass and crackling rhythm.

Below, a curdling farrago
of perfume, stout and sweat;

above: a bulb, a blood-light, sly
and brazen in the soft-edged dark.

DENISE SAUL

SCENT OF SEX

My summer dress hangs inside a wardrobe,
Its satin folds swell with the shape of me.
I rub my fingers on the shiny nub
of a button carved from mother-of-pearl.
The collar smells of cedarwood mothballs.

We are both ten. My cousin from Kansas
wears the same ivory dress. Our starched bows
stick out behind us as small angel wings.
After art-class, we run home on damp grass.
Dandelion seeds stick to our sandals.

My best friend climbs the old rowan tree.
She tucks her gingham pinafore inside
her pants as confetti of deep russet
and burgundy leaves fall on her shoulders.
Her plaited hair smells of crushed berries.

Years on, my oldest cousin wears white.
Her bridal gown unfolds on the aisle as
a lily heavy with scent of its sex.
As I hold her veil, pollen stains my hand.

SUDEEP SEN

Two extracts from a prose poem sequence
DREAMING OF CEZANNE

from
III. FOG

It is late afternoon. I gravitate towards anything that is warm –
smoke, steam, fire. I also gravitate towards colour, specific colours
– inhabiting the tactility of blue and the transparent imagination of
crimson.

I am attired in blue. I am in a room that is full of blue – blue linen,
blue curtains, blue oil painting, blue bottles, blue crayons.

Then I see red – pure red emerging from crimson on thick vellum.
A hand traces out an outline in ink – frenetic and spontaneous – red
lines highlighting the psychology of a face.

It is curious that I am encountering only the end-colours of the
spectrum – first blue-indigo-violet, and now predominantly red with
all its variant shades. It is a colour most unlikely to figure in this bleak
weather of neutrality, but it is omnipresent – red hair, red wool, red
petals, red moths, red candles, red fox, red soup, red fire, and red
eyes.

The retreat had begun with a pronouncement – pink irises dictating
grammar to our quills and its breathing. Now, nearly at the end of our
time – pink, crimson, lilac, and red – have revealed intricate space
and distance within each molecule of the original pigment.

IV. ROOMS

DINING ROOM

Pinkish-red beetroot soup, thick like chilled blood, was set in front of us in old pewter bowls. It smelled fresh and neutral, and all the crimson indications must have had a heavy price attached to them – there is "such finality about reality" [Arthur Miller].

I spangled the soup's foreskin with large flakes of fresh glint-edged pepper – the topsoil sprinkled this way added weight to its generous composure.

It was a formal evening, and the sacrifice was about to begin.

An errant butterfly, mistaking day for night, came fluttering into the room accidentally. She possessed a flap of desperation in the spring-folds of her wings. She flew around tentatively, randomly visiting each one of us, tasting the wet lips of the red-filled bowls in a vain attempt to keep alive –

A S Byatt's *Angels and Insects* seemed like an appropriate fantasy, as did Matisse's 'Blue Nude' sequence, and Cézanne's ever-returning presence –

This was live action – a butterfly trapped for human entertainment, a cruel beginning of another act in this staged drama.

It had to happen sooner or later – this beautiful insect took one last grand sweep of the night's artificial air, plunged, tracing her flight-path with its illuminated trail scripting the penultimate line of her epitaph with an electric streak that disappeared as soon as it appeared.

Then down she went, into the cold red of the soup — juice and juice, blood and blood — a heady, toxic communion.

A woman covered in russet wool tried to breathe in some life into the perishing wings. With anointed silver spoon, she scooped her out as she struggled to resuscitate herself in the dense froth, flapping desperately in slow motion.

Then it was time for the last rites — the butterfly in her open silver coffin was carried outside to her transparent grave, the night's cold air.

WINTER

Couched on crimson cushions,
  pink bleeds gold

and red spills into one's heart.
  Broad leather keeps time,

calibrating different hours
  in different zones

unaware of the grammar
  that makes sense.

Only random woofs and snores
  of two distant dogs

on a very cold night
  clears fog that is unresolved.

New plants wait for new heat –
  to grow, to mature.

An old cane recliner contains
  poetry for peace – woven

text keeping comfort in place.
  But it is the impatience of want

that keeps equations unsolved.
  Heavy, translucent, vaporous,

split red by mother tongues –
  winter's breath is pink.

ALMAYA, JAFFA
for Ya'ir Dalal

I like to keep my doors open —
It is like sitting in the desert —

   Under studio's arched ceiling flutes,
roof-paint uncoats, peeling lime white.
   Reverberating invisible sounds —
oud and violin, and a lone desert voice.

   Outside, the sea picks up its waves
in harmony. Inside, there are red
   oriental rugs, an uncleared stage
with notes from a concert past,

   kettle for sage tea, Iraqi sweets,
bottles of various shapes, and chairs —
   lots of mismatched chairs
like relatives from different tribes.

I like to keep my doors open —
It is like sitting in the desert —

   "Two flaming loves can burn you,"
you say. A Japanese girl
   who once heard you at a WOMAD
concert in Australia stumbles

   past your door, then stops
to look inside. "Is that you —
   the one in the poster on your door,"
she asks. You nod humbly

in your oblique quiet way.
"Almaya" – the name of your space –
   is christened then – "the universe
that embraces the waters".

I like to keep my doors open –
It is like sitting in the desert –

   The calm of the desert,
the turbulence of the sea,
   the early whistling of winds
before a gathering storm,

   the Bedouin's elongated cry,
the brothers' lisping embrace –
   hand-woven cream pashima
shawl – all score the elements.

I like to keep my doors open –
It is like sitting in the desert –

SENI SENEVIRATNE

BLOOD RED DROWNING

They cut my mother. Saved our lives
in a sudden blast of light and cold air.

Hungry for warmth, I craved skin.
Was cradled under a glass quilt.

A pink blanket – for her baby's shroud?
Bloodstained prayers, too late to save?

Her fears sewn behind the scars,
she never found a way to tell.

Mine were mute. I carried them all
wrapped in tight bundles around my back,

crying for comfort, rocked to fitful sleep.
Wanted, nearly lost, rejected, overprotected.

Hero and villain of family stories,
I never found a way to make amends

to her, who never made amends to me
who both only needed to accept the pain,

blood red, in which we drowned.

AFTER QANA – JULY 30TH 2006

After fifty-four civilians, mostly children, were killed
in an Israeli air-strike on a village in South Lebanon

I saw the lunchtime news and now

my arms ache with the dead weight of children whose bodies,
one by one, out of the rubble, I have not carried.

My fingers clench against one shoulder and under the bent knees
of a dead girl whose body in pink pyjamas, I have not lifted –

her head thrown back, her eyes closed against the dust –
whose cold hand against my chest I have not felt.

Despair lands like a bloated pigeon on the acacia tree,
drags down delicate branches, scatters the leaves;

hope disappears over my garden wall like a dragonfly,
as the leaves of the Virginia creeper turn red too soon

and underneath the trellis where the jasmine creeps,
the buddleia drips with purple tears and the butterflies don't care.

GRANDAD'S INSULIN

Nineteen fifty-five. I am four years old.
The tablecloth is flecked with crumbs and
smudged with teatime sauce. The cupboard's closed
on piles of jumbled toys and the silent wireless
stares down on me with pale eyes.

Knees and bottom cling to the comfy feel
of well-worn carpet's swirls – gold on red.
My legs fanned out on either side, I trace
one finger, seeking out smooth islands
where the pile has left this tufted ocean.

The old man breathing in a high green chair
has hands like my dad, but his eyes are browner
and his hair is greyer. He came last night with
stories, presents, kisses to cover my shyness.
I don't know him. My grandad from Ceylon.

He has a box today. Black. Leather. And when
he leans, those hands like my father's
click the silver lock, flip the lid. The treasure
of red lining pulls my finger off its course
towards the feel of velvet.

I rub, in steady, solid, up-and-down, side-to-side
strokes. The way it smooths and roughs itself
on my skin. I try not to look at the needle on a tube,
like in my brother's doctor set, but bigger.
Try to keep my eyes on the carpet,

so I won't follow his hands, like my father's,
as they raise the needle high above me.
Try to pull my eyes back to the velvet
to the red, where my finger's motion
is steadying me, so I won't see

the brown of his skin, as he dabs with cotton wool,
or the plunge of the needle, that makes my finger
stop short. And a voice like mine from far away
shouts *Oh* as my eyes squeeze themselves tight,
trying to see his ship coming over the sea

from a place I've only seen in picture books,
or the white blonde walking-doll he brought me,
but all I see is the needle piercing his skin.

JOHN SIDDIQUE

ASH MOON

Venus in the morning sky, fainter
at twilight. The Ash Moon, a chopping blade
moving closer to earth. Her gravity pulling the yellow
crocus heads to attention, moving cold
sap through the veins.

The ideas I've held onto for nearly ten years
seem thin in the clear light. Jupiter increases,
his storms are old, my storms are old.
There is no new again. There is now and however.

Your cards reply to my letter; it is time
to finish things. Time to stop trying
to impose order. Saturn is east of the Sun.

I cut the cards into four, light them in a candle flame.
Mix sage with the ash for cleanness, for clarity.
Not burning your names, but releasing the lives
we've imposed order on. The salsa band plays,
no one is dancing, the band haven't got anything else.

Hang red ribbon strips on the door posts.
Coins wrapped in red paper, given to the kids
for prosperity. The smoke releases us to new paths.
The white sage makes the imposition a choice.
The wind tossed Moon cuts up the stars.
Sagittarius is running ahead of the morning.

PROMISES

My wrists are burnt and bleeding, Chinese burns,
rope burns, pressure marks. I do the same for you
with each of these words, each word a knot
as we play *shibari* without the safety word.
Each promise a loss of the sensual.

We try to hold together, bind our lives into
what we'd like to be. Darling, we change ourselves
into each other's ideas, ceasing to be the fire,
the excitement we were for each other
in syllabic increments.

Tied up in red, in elegant silk,
in gorgeous words. Tied up, trying. Tied up, losing
our lives whilst making tourniquets of these ropes;
the bondage of need, desire and loneliness.

Cycle

cotton

moody

white

lunar

stains

face

blood

tears

sheets

LEMN SISSAY

WINTER: SHEPHERD'S WARNING

The clothes on the wash-line, limp and still,
A renegade spit of rain races through enemy lines
And crashes on a dustbin lid. Telltale signs.
Echoes ricochet around the estate in opposite directions,
Alsatians run in circles chasing their tails.
Confused birds fall with wings of sycamore seeds.
She creeps carefully with menace wrapped in cloak of silence,
Twisting in the scowling face, the breathless body,
The weakening pulse of the sky.
Hold onto your children or they'll be swept away
Down the dark rivers of your High Street
Or dragged by the wind up the sides of skyscrapers –
Red sky of a morning, shepherd's warning.

This wind wades through the waves of the sky
And marches onto blood-spattered beaches towards us.
Her bitter breath in the strains of air. Cold chills spill.
Sound the alarm. Hold onto your loved ones.
Call your friends, tell them, *Don't come around. Stay in.*
There are disappearances in Dogger.
Raging seas in Rockall.

She will slip into the houses, crawl the stairs of the frail,
Grip necks as we sleep. She will suffocate them.
I hear the choking sound of the hidden. The rain applauds.
Grown trees crackle, snap and whip as wooden coffins
Squeeze through nervous doors,
Spades plunge into the crisp fresh of earth.
Red sky of a morning – shepherd's warning.

The veins of the sky have burst.
Weather reporters are in flak jackets.

Cliffs with their chests plucked out cry wet stone tears
Into the panicking and frantic sea.
Trees with their hair pulled towards the sky have
Innards torn out and cut from the ground. Take your children.
The storm is here. The storm is here. The storm is here.

Thunder preaches from the pulpit, faces leak
From the brilliant cracks in the sky, lunging
Spiked arms. The end is nigh! The end is nigh!
All the christs and all the gods have been released,
All the devils and all the demons and
All the plagues and all the diseases, and all the spirits
And all the ghosts. Released. Released. Released.

Keep your windows closed. Wrap up warm.
And fall into dreams in this mantra, hugging plastic bottles
Of boiling water, through dreams of swimming in tears.
And the tears become the dark leaves of autumn
And the dark leaves become wet tongues and the wet tongues
A storm-filled sea. In the morning when my neck bursts
Through the surface and I grasp for breath, a bright warm light
Punches through my darkness, there is nothing but a reddened battlefield
Of a sky and the muffled sounds of flocks and shepherds.
Red sky in the morning – shepherd's warning.

DOROTHEA SMARTT

RED MUDDER

When the message come thru
Daddy first woman gone,
I couldn't help thinking how she outlive he long.
She was a cord to he pas' life, he life before me,
a young fellah 'bout Bridgetown circa 1933.

Not long after he pass, I went out to meet her,
ask she all 'bout Daddy –
and any memories that keep her.
She pass way now and all she stories gone
but the Red Mudder did pass summa dem on.

The Red Mudder, common-law,
tell me all 'bout Daddy young boy days,
the fella she fall fuh, the kinda faader he made.
She still had the 'Singer', but he goat long gone.
Even one o' she dawter dead, lef ' she an' gone long.

Daddy was a man like nuff women –
so she tell me, as we went 'long!
But she feel she was he red queen,
and with he mudder on the scene,
she was not like dem others at-all.

She bring out de ole Bible, where he write up
all their children names –
the Bible sen from London,
widda picture of he 'bout Town,
pidgins bustlin' 'bout Nelson's Column
and this Bay Street boy. See
he really arrive now!

Then there was he old passport pic –
he, widda moustache, I never see that yet!
She, in she good-dress, mek up the night before –
it had a red sash, and small red bows.
De hat was de ting – Daddy sen it from London (de Motherlan')
and de dress she make to match.
Lives they live before I even hatch.

When the message come thru
Daddy first woman gone,
I couldn't help thinking how she outlive he long
She was a cord to his pas' life, he life before me,
a young fellah 'bout Bridgetown in 1933.

RED

After Walter de la Mare's 'Silver'

Racing rapidly, now the car
streaks the night with her red stars
heading away. It slides and careens,
red lights on red trees.
One by one each roadside shack
the red beam makes a red catch.
Crouched by the verge, like a log
with paws of red a guarding dog;

From their wintry coats the red breasts peep,
robins in a red-feathered sleep.
A nocturnal fox goes gliding by
with red hindfoot after red eye.
A motionless salmon in the rear light gleam
by red reeds in a red stream.

ROMMI SMITH

BILLIE'S FUR COAT

Billie's wearing dollars
on her broadest shoulders;
Billie's rich on fur, making it look
like carrying the weight of half the sky
upon your head –
is just a two-dime tightrope balancing act.

Watch.

Billie's feeling flush on third-night applause,
Billie rolling smokes made from blank cheques.
Billie's silk, like moon against her skin.
A stranger casts his eyes and orders – gin.

But,

Billie's mood is ready for champagne;
the fur across her back could be alive
to howl to him of all the tears she saved –
to pay for these moments to arrive.

So,

Billie stands beside him. Waiting. Waiting,
(she thinks) to receive the thrown rose
of his compliment, not the vicious tip
promised by a drunk, nor gin's deliberate perfume on her
coat.

"Nigger," he says, as a final act.

In

these anonymous times, I like
to think that she said something
for us all that night. I'm sure that
his face wore the shape of countless,
soulless men, who had betrayed her;
her father, lovers.

I

think of all the lies he told
when he got home: the guy
he taught a lesson; the man
he'd scarred for fun,
how, despite the evidence
written on his face in blood –

he'd won.

SARADHA SOOBRAYEN

WITH LOVE FROM RUSSIA

In an exchange of letters
the word for red: *Krassny,*
became very close to *Krassivy*,
the word for beautiful.

VERMILLION'S SPEECH

I, Vermillion, was created with excellent
hiding powers, a pigment with good
permanence. With a history of cardinals'
robes and an aversion to light, I curse thee,
boils, pox, a plague on your canvases.
Purified and scorched, I *Vermeilion*
am not lust on a palate knife, fire-hair
wrestling with the snake, Adam turning
back to clay, his apple the colour of Mars.
Vermiculus: a rash worm flying in the night,
volatile cochineal by day. *Vermiglio*, crushed
like grapes between lips the size of peonies.
How I yearn to become less of an exercise
in desire, and seep into white, unnoticed.

BLEED

Imagine marking skin
with a red felt-tip pen,
skin cooling against zinc.

Lines itching into shapes
and negative spaces,
stains of copper oxide

decreasing contours,
a left breast, an oval,
a brush slapping yellows;

too late, too late, curves
losing curves, keeping scars
under a slow bruise,

shades of madder dribbling
from the cut, lines left
unwashed, dyeing skin.

TINA TAMSHO-THOMAS

COPPER COLOURED HAIR

A small group
of brightly dressed women
sit on a low church wall,
their laughter mingling
with sounds of traffic.

One swings the heel
of her stylish stiletto
in time to the rhythm
of her racing thoughts.

One sits sideways
displaying thigh-high boots,
to a passing down-and-out
whose sad grey eyes
hold only memories.

Another looks anxiously
at her watch,
the face she sees reflected there,
a stark reminder of the price
we all must pay.

But the one
with copper coloured hair,
lips and nails,
stares straight ahead
and she
simply...
smiles.

MARVIN THOMPSON

BURIED

The darkness, the red boots, the blood moon
and all I hear is the strange beat of my heart,
feel it drumming in my wrists.

I could say sorry, goodbye, lie about an empty wallet.
The massage is first, soft palms and baby powder,

every image of Dawn drowned,
my heartbeat slowing to match the rhythm of the waves,
Dawn pulling me deeper into her heart,

her sweat rising, vodka and coke sweet on her lips
and if I tell her now there'll be so much death.

Tumblers lie strewn on the hotel floor.
Outside the sea's singing. She asks,
Have you been here before?

I lie, say nothing. She asks if I love her.
I say yes. I'm close enough. But not touching.

AMBER

Her fingers are the colour of raw
unpeeled, red roasting-potatoes. They look
as though she scratches them until they're sore.
Today she's browsing the cookery books,
trying to find a present for her friend's
birthday. I stare at her boots, maroon
leather disappearing up the hemmed
legs of her Levis. Paul bought macaroons
from the local patisserie. I should
offer her one. Or maybe I should ask
if she minds me ogling her shoulders.
Is that ring on her wedding finger? Last
time she came in I spent the week in dream-
land, where we kissed, held hands, shared ice cream.

KIMBERLY TRUSTY

FIREWORKS, NEW CROSS ROAD, 1981

There were fireworks
pink and white star shower
green and gold clouds
the night I met you
New Year's Eve 1980
we watched the night sky spark up
from behind the glass
of a shop front window

A bashment in a Brixton record shop
I was trendy and tragic
in skinny, paint-splattered jeans
and battered Nike high tops
my hair wet and curly
like Coco from *Fame*

You? you were all
roots   rock   rebel
baby dreads sticking out
from your head like a satellite
army fatigues and a red
"black market Clash" t-shirt
you held out a record sleeve
asked if I liked Black Uhuru

I sipped my beer and wondered
if you could tell from the crinkle
between my eyebrows that
the last record I bought
was "We got the beat" by the Go-Go's
thank God for fireworks
those pyrotechnic fireflies

A year later
we celebrate your 21ˢᵗ birthday
at a friend's house in
New Cross Road where
two girls, Angela and Yvonne,
are also celebrating birthdays
we are antisocial socialisers
standing in a corner in the front room
alone together in a room full of people

I know who Black Uhuru are now
and sometimes I catch you singing
the *Fame* theme song under your breath
when you think I'm busy with something else
random velocities of our molecules
have made us one

The glow from red paper Chinese lanterns
takes the sharpness out of your cheekbones
we hold each other tight and rock
to "Gauva Jelly" unaware that the Lion is ailing
my fingers twisted in
your shoulder-length locks
the heat from your body a spark
that sets off fireworks in the pit of my stomach

And then…

I see red.
Not from paper lanterns.
I see orange.
Not from 21 candles on your cake.
I feel heat.
Not from your body.

And it is red and orange and heat and people running and young women screaming and it's then that I lose you, get carried out in a wave of colour and noise. Still hot from your body and the party and the… I don't notice New Year cold. I move from person to person, grabbing at jumpers, t-shirts and coats, screaming above the scream-ing and the fire and the sirens, "Where is he? Have you seen him?" but no one answers. I see fireworks behind my eyes, trip over someone prone in the street and sit down heavily on the pavement. I scream so loudly and so long that a lifetime passes. A lifetime passes before I notice your arms around me and although you're whispering my name I can hear it above the screaming and the fire and the sirens and my own sobs because we share molecules; are one.

My Coco curls are smoke and ash
your dreads are singed, your 21st year a house on fire
but energy is kinetic; our molecules' random velocity
and we are one

And the following day?
the following day we are one
one with the 13 dead
one with the 20 injured
one with the 15,000 people
who take to the streets
and put a too silent police force
on notice

Our fear
our anger
our sorrow
our determination
our new awareness
diffuses across the nation
and we are one

WANGŨI WA GORO

RHAPSODY IN PINK, OR JUST "BISSAP"

Imagine what flights of fancy can yield,
Flight, by firelight,
Fireflight, flight fleeting,
Fleetingly feeling flighty,
Free,
In freeform
Falling,
Falling like leaves in the autumn,
Flying in the winds,
Flailing their wings
Helplessly,
Joyously,
Freely,
Fleeing in feckless freedom.

Imagine altered egos,
Altered comings and goings,
In morning rhapsody,
Mango,
Bissap,
Juices flowing
Rhapsody in pink.

Mmm… morning glory
Rhapsody in blue and white where major and minor meet

Even in evensong, orange and red

The lustre and timbre of words still linger on the tongue.

Imagine the night of a million stars and a trillion dreams

The galaxy and the Milky Way

Imagine the distances we could travel if we imagine.

Just imagine

A WATERY SUMMER SONG

I

Water, everywhere I go,
love warm came bouncing at me
in large waves
and varied hues,
flowing in action
engulfing me
Thirsty for life
I travel
in search of the greater muses,
I see here the great bear, hug
of one, Egejuru, no, two
Osundare
from New Orleans.
Their tears not yet dry
enfold me,
water and tides and seasons
all. Oh the distance to Macomb and Na'Allah
that I travel to meet my poet, warrior sister
sojourner, who has made me feel
as I sip, my lips full
beads of bi Kidude's words
as she rides her drum
far away from where we hid our umbilicals,
which we vowed to retrieve
here North!
Awed by the great halls of gold
which held our Nobelic Greenbelt Queen
our eyes meet:
Shailja in Migrations girations, tigrations, I, in jubilation, rejuvenation.
Kivuitu
answers her,

still he will not go.
I her hand will not let go

II

I will sail further south
wearing my earrings that Kassahun from Eritrea
gave me in Peoria celebrating 25 –
while chastising me in whisper:
"Not even a poem for me?" –
forged from amber
bright and red like the Sea Press
in Adinkra symbol
gye nyame,
pampering my face, in the long memory
of when we met in London.
Ringing my cancer head
to reveal the flowing beauty
of our long 25 years in friendship
candle-lit by a thousand books,
YOU light my path

III

Home bound to my mother queen
from New Orleans, Phanuel;
"Baby" she calls me.
I bow as she comes to restore me,
restore her, in farewell to New Orleans,
that place of jazz and woes.
Sailing down the Thames we swell
salient
our colonial/present memory
smiling

IV

Two "shebeen queens" go sailing
down Lake Geneva,
saluted by the magnificent Alps in glory,
laughing till water runs down and down
from everywhere. I swear
at *Ubuntu*'s wicked jokes,
at the waiter who assures us that he
is married.

V

I am southward bound
and lie in Centurion's drying lake,
not far from John Vorster Square:
a summer full of so many memories,
such blood and water
gushing,
mesmeric poetry and love.
"I just can't forget the past",
Biko's and Bika's voices
whisper to me
here, from beyond the grave

VI

And your love?
How long will it flutter
like amniotic mystery?
I cannot fathom
how we ate Indian sweets,
halva and jalebi,
in the cemetery
under the watchful eyes of Christ,
where the gravestones have been moved

and we will not remember who stood where
to mourn the dead,
where we will all procession
some day.
And still you have not moved?

VII

Latent love is wonderful,
but that present love which visits
far greater.
Come feed my embrace
with ackee or salt fish,
curry goat or rice and peas, I care not.
Let us be thankful
and let it flow
for the summer tidings
in this mysterious land
of poetic showers.

KAVERI WOODWARD

WEB

Moths play round the security light.

For once the kitchen table is clean.
Our lives stacked in the dishwasher,
whilst letters rustle across a page.
I don't recognise the writing
or even the whispered words. They say:
a bad workman always blames his tools.
But you refuse to be used.
In the hard darkness, I sit alone.

Moths play round the security light.

A red sequin gleams on the carpet,
confetti from our daughters' games.
No more romantic than the toast crumbs
and soft dust bunnies under our chairs.
Beneath the lamp's cool phosphorus,
we have lost life's one mystery,
its secret blown away
with the grey shreds from my eraser.

Moths play round the security light.

GEMMA WEEKES

FIRST COLOUR FOR BEAU

Slung low,
Cradled soft,
Making home.
A brand-new someone
Is liquid suspended is
A jewel acquiring layers
Bone
By bone,
By nerve,
By cell.

A love poem of flesh,
Free of past or future,
Now and now and now
And now!

Baby's first colour is
Eyelid,
Is *warm.*
First colour is muffled
Singing,
Sweet vibration through
Tiny, transparent body.

The everything is happy!

Somersaults
With no hard landings.
No *hard.*
What is hard?

First colour is soft rhythm

On and on,
Hollow thump of *everything*
Is baby's first taste of religion.

Something that is
Not him?

Building himself brand new!
A skin has grown over
The old life.
Now
There is no *old.*

All is one sweet colour!
Safe here.
Fun in all the warm!
What is *cold?*

(Hmm...)

Nourishment is
Sometimes one way
Sometimes an *other!*

One does not... *like...*
Them all!

Getting stronger! Practise
To get strong but –

Once One could do somersaults!
Now so strong
One is *big* as the *whole* of everything!
One has one's own *thump-thump-thump*
Like the everything!

Is One *one* with
The everything?

Or is The Everything an
Other thing?

An *other* one!

(Hmm…)

Once One had space to kick one's
Legs but now there is *none*!
Once one had space to kick one's
Legs but now there is *none*! Once one had space to kick one's
Legs but now there is *none*! *None! None! None!*
What a hot squash.
(Hmm…!)

First colour is red.

First word is *now*.
Second word is…

Soon…?

(Hmm…
Mmm…
Mmm… aaaah
Mmm… AAAH!)

(FOUND POEM)
(*mostly*)

how you write red
human observer?
see, feel the adjective
end of the visible (redder, reddest)
a colour at the end

spectrum next to orange
opposite violet the hue of the
long-wave spectrum,
embarrassment, anger smell

love?
hate?
how you write red?
jealous is red
Not –

(That is up to you.)

red
toss turn pull
we want you, red poem!

deliver
definition red!

evoked in
radiant energy wavelengths?
(That is also up to you.)

psychological primary hues.
how you write red?

any colours
may vary in lightness

one of the additive or light primaries;
saturation
is blood always red?

as of fire
rubies, heat?
How you write red!

Up to you.
Up to you.
Up to you.

NOTES

p. 29 ("Infinity in Red"): *gulmohur* – royal poinciana or flamboyant tree, also called flame of the forest.

sanka – a shell (turbinella pyrum) often made into a bracelet.

p.48 ("Unity"): *lwa* – loa; gods or ancestor spirits.

Ginen – Guinea, or more generally a mythical place of African origins.

Gede – spirits who are guardians of the dead and masters of sexual desire.

Petro – the lwa associated with violent, implacable forces, death and harm; one of the systems within Haitian voodoo.

p. 51 ("Red Robber"): *red robber* – the midnight robber of carnival, character-ised by extravagant costume and boastful, bombastic, hyperbolic speech.

p. 55 ("Kali Mirchi"): *kali mirchi* – Punjabi for black pepper.

p. 56 ("Spurn"): *khana* – solid food; *pani* – water.

p. 104 ("Five Nights of Bleeding"): *Leroy Harris* – a victim of internecine violence.

shepherds – Methodist Youth Club on Railton Road, named after the first youth leader.

rainbow – a former music venue in Finsbury Park, London.

telegraph – a public bar on Brixton Hill where reggae was played in the early 1970s.

pp. 107-116 ("Bougainvillea: Super 8 Red"): *moko-jumbie* – a carnival mas player on stilts, of West African origin.

obatala – Orisha supreme being or creator.

burrokeets – a carnival mas player representing a donkey and rider.

jab molassie – a carnival devil covered in molasses, pitch oil or mud.

sans humanité – a stickfighter's or calypsonian's cry (literally *No mercy!*).

gilpin – a long cutlass with a curved end (as made by W.S. Gilpin of Stafford).

cosquelle – dressed in loud, garish colours.

dame lorraine – a usually cross-dressed carnival character, originally burlesquing French plantation wives.

p. 129 ("The Visit"): See the Old Testament, "Judith 13: 2" – Judith and Holofernes.

p. 135 ("Red Diamonds"): *lambada* – a semi-nomadic tribe of various groups

236

found in most parts of India although most of them are found in Andhra Pradesh, a state in the south east of India.

pp. 137-139 ("Sure, Reds"): *akoko* – fowl cock (West African origin).

bois-fighter – stick fighter, martial arts of Afrikan origin in the Caribbean, from 1800s in Trinidad.

jamette – regarded by the colonial authorities as rowdy or promiscuous women. These women would lead riots.

babash – an illegally brewed rum.

spiritual baptist – Christian sect influenced by African traditions.

Hosay – Muslim Festival of Muharram.

sun – a large Hosay head-dress, weighing many kilos.

djab – devil.

jouvert – early morning Carnival (from French Patois).

Maurice – assassinated Prime Minister Maurice Bishop of Grenada.

PRG – Peoples Revolutionary Government of Grenada.

red house – Parliament of Trinidad & Tobago. It was painted red to celebrate the Diamond Jubilee of Queen Victoria and was thus nicknamed by locals as the Red House.

coup – in 1990 the Muslimeen, a radical Islamic group, invaded the Parliament of Trinidad & Tobago and held MPs hostage in an attempted coup.

stained glass – During the Water Riots of 1903 (when 13 protesters were killed by the colonial police), a stained glass window to commemorate the arrival of Christopher Columbus erected in the Parliament Chamber of the Red House was smashed and part of the building destroyed by fire.

Sir Cornelius Alfred Moloney – Governor of Trinidad & Tobago from 1901-1904.

Ineri – indigenous peoples of Trinidad.

roucou – fruit indigenous to Trinidad used in food colouring; originally used by Ineri to ritually paint their skin.

Sangre Grande – town named after massacre of Spanish Capuchin missionaries.

Holi – Hindu Spring Festival. *Holi* is celebrated by Hindus by the singing of special songs called chowtaals and by the spraying of coloured powder (*abrack*) and dyed water (*abeer*).

parang – Caribbean folk music genre, with its origins in Trinidad. It is closely associated with Christmas festivities and traditionally comes from the Spanish word "parranda" (action of merry making, group of serenaders).

La Divina Pastora – festival of a rescued statue: "The Divine Shepherdess" in Siparia, Trinidad. This tradition is also very common in Spain and Hispanic America.

soca warriors – T&T football Team who qualified for 1996 World Cup.

oui – we or alternatively yes or our.

wine – the gyrating of the waist – Caribbean dancing.

PNM – Peoples National Movement (political party).

CoP – Congress of the People (political party).

de real RED – the leaders of CoP boasted that they will display "de real red" in a rally for the upcoming elections.

UNC – United National Congress (political party).

p. 140 ("Red, as red as you like"): *lamasery* – Tibetan religious centre.

p. 142 ("Arrival"): *rassam* – Rassam is a popular Tamil soup known as 'pepper water'. Made with pepper, jeera, cardamom, garlic, onions, tamarind and water.

p. 143 ("Breathing Palm Oil"): *suya joint* – (Nigerian) roadside restaurant serving *suya*, skewered, spiced grilled meat.

nyash – buttocks.

p. 145 ("Sugar Cane Bundown"): *bullpistle* – whip made of a bull's penis.

p. 172 ("I want"): *isiqwabalanda* – (Ndebele) thugs.

p. 178 ("Stripping Yam"): *kelewele* – spiced, soft, deep-fried bite-sized morsels of plantain.

yele – yam.

p. 206 ("Promises"): *Shibari* – the art of Japanese bondage.

p. 224 ("Rhapsody in Pink or Just Bissap"): *bissap* – a kind of hibiscus from which a drink is made (like sorrel).

p. 226 ("A Watery Summer Song"): *Egejuru* – Phanuel Akubueze Egejuru, Nigerian writer and critic, based in New Orleans.

Osundare – Niyi Osundare, Nigerian poet, dramatist and essayist.

bi Kidude – Zanzibari Taarab singer and drummer, a woman of great age.

Shailja – Shailja Patel, Kenyan poet, author of *Migritude*.

Kivuitu – Samuel Kivuitu, chairman of the Kenyan electoral commission during disputed elections.

Kassahun – Kassahun Checole, publisher of Africa World Press and Red Sea Press.

Ubuntu – a women's group dedicated to combatting sexual violence.

CONTRIBUTORS

Abdullahi Botan Hassan "Kurweyne" was born in Somalia in 1969 and started composing poems as a teenager. He came to London in 1998 and has become well known for his poems based on his experience there. In 2003 he founded Soohan Somali Arts which works with Somali children in primary schools in Camden.

Martin Orwin (translator for Abdullahi Botan Hassan "Kurweyne") was born in 1963. He is Senior Lecturer in Somali and Amharic at the School of Oriental and African Studies in London where he teaches these languages. He has published articles on Somali poetry, in particular on the metrical system and the way language is used.

Sylvia Jean Abrahams grew up as Cape Coloured during apartheid, dancing in the streets below Table Mountain. Her multi-ethnic identities shape her writing. Recently divorced, her untamed African spirit survives in Sussex. She has a creative writing MA from Chichester University and is published in the *Decibel Penguin Anthology*, *Volume I*. kapiesyl@hotmail.com

Shanta Acharya was born in India, educated at Oxford and Harvard, currently lives in London. Of her five books of poetry, the latest is *Dreams that Spell the Light* (Arc Publications, 2009). Her doctoral study, *The Influence of Indian Thought on Ralph Waldo Emerson*, was published by The Edwin Mellen Press, USA. www.shantaacharya.com

John Agard was born in Guyana. He has several collections for children and adults, including *Man To Pan* which won the 1983 Casa de las Americas Poetry Award and *We Brits* (Bloodaxe Books) which was shortlisted for the Arts Council Decibel Award. His latest Bloodaxe collection is *Clever Backbone*, a sequence of sonnets inspired by evolution.

Patience Agbabi was born in London and educated at Oxford and Sussex Universities. Renowned for her live performances, her poems have been broadcast all over the world. She has lectured in Creative Writing at several UK universities. Her latest collection is *Bloodshot Monochrome* (Canongate, 2008). www.57productions.com

Ebele Ajogbe is a Nigerian-brown East-Londoner surviving on mangoes, dreams… and, erm, Body Shop Coconut Body Butter. Writing since 2002, her work veers from earthy to playful to surreal. She has performed at the Glastonbury Festival, on BBC Radio 3, in Paradiso (Amsterdam) and many venues across the UK.
www.ebele.co.uk

Mir Mahfuz Ali was born in Dhaka, Bangladesh. He studied at Essex University and has performed at the Royal Opera House and elsewhere. His work is published in *London Magazine*, *Poetry London* and *Ambit*. He was shortlisted for a New Writing Venture Award 2007. Mahfuz's first collection of poetry is in preparation.

Moniza Alvi is a freelance writer and tutor. Her first five collections were reprinted in *Split World: Poems 1990-2005* (Bloodaxe Books, 2008). *The Country at My Shoulder* was shortlisted for the T.S. Eliot and Whitbread poetry prizes, and *Carrying My Wife* was a Poetry Book Society Recommendation. *Europa* was shortlisted for the T.S. Eliot Prize in 2008.

Bibi is a Nigerian born Londoner. She has been writing off and on (more off than on) since 2000 and has published three volumes of poetry and prose: *Love Notes*, *Limited Edition: Woman*, and *Terms of Endearment,* all published by Author House.
www.poetryismusic.co.uk

Maroula Blades is an Afro-British writer living in Berlin. *Verbrecher Verlag* and *Cornelsen Verlag* have published her short stories. She has received awards for poetry. Poems have been published in Germany and abroad. She read at the Berlin Poetry Festival 2008, and was the featured poet in the *Erbacce 16*.

Malika Booker is a British writer of Guyanese and Grenadian parentage, who writes poetry. She has also written for the stage and radio. Her one-woman show, "Unplanned", toured nationwide throughout 2007 and her poetry collection *Breadfruit* was published by flipped eye in 2007, She is currently working on her first full length collection. http://tinyurl.com/2ecb6t

Mark Angelo de Brito is a poet, translator and critic. Two of his books have been published by Peepal Tree Press: *Heron's Canoe* (2003, original poetry) and *The Trickster's Tongue* (2007, poetic translations). He lives in London.

Faustin Charles is a poet, storyteller, children's writer and dramatist. He has also edited several anthologies. He is the author of the best selling classic children's book *The Selfish Crocodile* which has now sold half a million copies. His work has appeared in anthologies in England, America, Europe and the Caribbean. Peepal Tree published *Children of the Morning: Selected Poems* in 2008.

Debjani Chatterjee MBE is an Indian-born poet, editor, translator and children's writer. She is also a Royal Literary Fund Fellow, Co-Chair of Hyphen 21... and Patron of Survivors' Poetry. Her many books include *Namaskar: New & Selected Poems* and *Words Spit and Splinter*, both from Redbeck Press.

Maya Chowdhry is a poet and inTer-aCtive artist; a winner of the Cardiff International poetry competition, her poetry appears in *The Seamstress and the Global Garment*, *Healing Strategies for Women at War*, *Ambit* and *The Popular Front of Contemporary Poetry*. She received an ACE literature award for her poetic web tapestry – www.destinynation.net/poetree/

Joseph Coelho is a poet and playwright. He runs inspirational creative writing workshops all over the country. He has had poems published by Macmillan and the Southbank Centre and he has a new collection coming out with flipped eye publishing in early 2010. He is a board member of literature organisation, Spread the Word.

Fred D'Aguiar's sixth collection of poems, *Continental Shelf* (Carcanet, 2009) was a Poetry Book Society Summer Choice. His fifth novel, *Bethany Bettany* was published in 2003. He teaches at Virginia Tech where he is Gloria D. Smith Professor of Africana Studies and Professor of English.

Martin De Mello is a poet and fiction writer. He has played a leading role in the development of a community of black poets in Manchester. He teaches an advanced black poets course and an advanced fiction course through Cultureword.

Imtiaz Dharker is an artist and documentary film-maker, and has published four books with Bloodaxe, *Postcards from god* (including "Purdah") (1997), *I speak for the devil* (2001), *The terrorist at my table* (2006) and *Leaving Fingerprints* (2009); all include her own drawings. She lives between India, London and Wales.

Lizzy Dijeh is a playwright and poet. In 2001 she won the London Writers Competition's Promis Prize for poetry. She has had play readings in London theatres and the debut production of *High Life* was at Hampstead Theatre in October 2009. It was published by Oberon Books in 2009.

Tishani Doshi is a writer and a dancer of Welsh and Indian heritage, based in Madras, India. Her first book of poems, *Countries of the Body*, won the Forward Prize for Best First Collection in 2006. She has a novel forthcoming from Bloomsbury.

Jeanne Ellin has held residencies in a prison working with people convicted of serious sexual offences and in a hospice working with staff, patients and relatives. She has worked with South Asian teenagers with learning disabilities and people with dementia. Currently collaborating with a dark rock band on lyrics. *Who Asks the Caterpillar?* was published by Peepal Tree in 2004.

Crista Ermiya was one of the inaugural winners of the Decibel Penguin Short Story Prize (2006). She grew up in London, of Filipino and Turkish-Cypriot parentage and now lives in Newcastle-upon-Tyne.

Bernardine Evaristo's books include *Hello Mum* (Penguin 2010), *Lara* (Bloodaxe 2009), *Blonde Roots* (2008), *Soul Tourists* (2005) and *The Emperor's Babe* (2001). She has won several awards, is a Fellow of the Royal Society of Literature and was awarded an MBE for services to literature in 2009. www.bevaristo.net

Patricia Foster is an internationally published writer, performer, radio broadcaster and educator. She has performed poetry and theatre at many prominent London venues. She has also toured Europe and the USA, featured on Sky TV, Dutch and BBC Radio and collaborated with UK Jazz musicians. www.myspace.com/patriciafosterperformer

Jean Hall was born in Coventry in 1968 and educated at Ruskin College, Oxford and the London School of Oriental and African Studies. She enjoys drawing on the rich oral traditions of Africa and the Caribbean and relevant cultural and political themes in her work. Her work includes both poetry and prose.

Maggie Harris won the Guyana Prize 2000 for her first collection, *Limbolands.* A second collection, *From Berbice to Broadstairs*, was published in 2000. A performer, prose writer and teacher, her work has taken her to the Caribbean and Europe. As International Teaching Fellow at Southampton University, she has initiated Caribbean and Black British Writing into teacher training for secondary schools. www.maggieharris.co.uk

Louise Hercules is a London based artist who specialises in both poetry and photography. Louise's dynamic body of work explores provocative themes such as identity, gender and relationships through the use of sensual imagery and dramatic dialogue which permeate throughout her artwork.

Cyril Husbands is a storyteller, songwriter, poet and live artist. His work draws on his pan-Africanist and radical humanist politics, as well as history, memory and relationships. He seeks to inspire audiences and readers to think, act, reflect and imagine, as other writers and artists do for him.

Khadijah Ibrahiim is of Jamaican parentage, born in Leeds. She is the Artistic Director of Leeds Young Authors and executive producer of "Voices of a New Generation" Lit & Slam Festival. Her poetry chap book, *Rootz Runnin',* was published by Peepal Tree Press (2008), when she also toured the USA with the "Fwords: Creative Freedom" writers.

Joshua Idehen is the founder of the London based collective A Poem Inbetween People, the Afrofunk band, Benin City, and the successful poetry/music night Poejazzi. This year he wants to do more.

Linton Kwesi Johnson is known as the world's first reggae poet, starting his record label in 1981. He is the author of five poetry collections and the recipient of several awards and honorary doctorates. In 2002 he became only the second living poet and the first black poet to have his work published in Penguin's Modern Classics series, with *Mi Revalueshanary Fren*.

Anthony Joseph is a poet, novelist, scholar and musician. He was born in Trinidad, moving to the UK in 1989. His publications include *Desafinado*, *Teragaton*, *The African Origins of UFOs* and *Bird Head Son*. Joseph lectures in creative writing at Birkbeck College and at Goldsmiths College where he is a doctoral candidate. www.anthonyjoseph.co.uk

Peter Kalu is a poet, playwright and novelist. He has had six novels published and numerous radio and theatre plays produced. He is an editor for North West of England based publishers, Crocus and Suitcase Press. He writes under his own name as well as under several pseudonyms. Website: www.peterkalu.co.uk

Jackie Kay's *Darling: New and Selected Poems* was a Poetry Book Society Recommendation. Her most recent collection of short stories, *Wish I Was Here* won the Decibel Prize. She is Professor of Creative Writing at Newcastle University.

Alvin Kirby was born 1974 in London to Antiguan parents. He started writing poetry in his late teens after discovering West Indian writers. His poems explore cross-cultural themes, inspired by London, family and holidays "back home" to Antigua. He currently resides in Launceston, Tasmania, with his Australian wife and three children.

Usha Kishore was born and brought up in South India. She now lives on the Isle of Man, where she is Keystage 5 English Co-ordinator in a secondary school. Usha's poetry, short stories, translations from Sanskrit and critical articles have all been published internationally. She can be contacted at vajra@manx.net

Janet Kofi-Tsekpo has poetry and prose featured in *Bittersweet: Contemporary Black Women's Poetry*, *Wasafiri*, and other publications. She is currently on 'The Complete Works' programme run by Spread the Word, and the forthcoming anthology will be published by Bloodaxe.

Kokumo captures his audience with his performance skills, whilst taking them on a cultural, spiritual and political journey. This journey has taken him across the globe, championing social and cultural awareness, through the use of reggae and dub poetry. Kokumo is also described as an artist and a cultural anthropologist. www.myspace.com/kokumo

Vasundhara Kulkarni was born and raised in India, studied in the United States and then worked as a psychotherapist/counsellor in London at a South Asian Woman's Charity. She recently moved to Australia and continues to pursue writing as a hobby. She has penned several short stories and poems about her multicultural experiences.

Roi Ankhkara Kwabena (July 23, 1956 – January 9, 2008) was born in Trinidad. He moved to Britain in 1985 after political and cultural activity in Trinidad. He was a cultural activist – poet, musician, storyteller, historian and publisher. Roi was the sixth Poet Laureate for Birmingham, England (2001-2002). His last poetry collection is titled *Whether or Not.*
http://www.roikwabena.blogspot.com/

Judith Lal was born in the Cotswolds and now lives in Norwich. Her poems have appeared in various magazines. She has an MA in Creative Writing from the University of East Anglia. She received an Eric Gregory Award in 2001. Her pamphlet *Flageolets at the Bazaar* was chosen as a Poetry Book Society Recommendation.

Sundra Lawrence is a poet and literature entrepreneur. She has performed her work nationally and internationally. Sundra is the founder of the youth poetry project Write Lines. Her work has been broadcast on BBC 2 and is published in numerous anthologies including the *Los Angeles Review*. *Starchild* is her first mini-collection.

Segun Lee-French is a Nigerian Mancunian singer, poet, producer/composer, playwright, and film-maker, founder member of Manchester's Speakeasy People poetry collective. As poet and playwright, Segun's work has been broadcast on BBC Radio 3 and his debut solo show, "Bro:9", won Best Fringe Performer & Best Design in the MEN Theatre Awards 2003.

Dawn Saba Liburd is a Social Sciences Graduate with a Post Graduate Certificate in Education and Religious Studies. She has completed numerous studies in creative writing and her poetry has been described as 'visceral' and 'striking'. She is the founder of 'Natural Play' holistic childcare services and lives in London. www.facebook.com/people/Dawn-Liburd/1598923085

John Lyons, nationally recognised Trinidadian painter and poet, is twice winner of the Peterloo Poetry Competition and an Arvon Foundation tutor. His fourth collection is *Selected and New Poetry: No Apples in Eden*. His *Cook-Up in a Trini Kitchen,* recipes, poems, drawings and paintings was published by Peepal Tree in 2009. Website: www.johnlyons.org Link: www.ovendenart.com

Sheree Mack is the founder of identity on tyne and editor of several anthologies by ID on Tyne Press. Publications include special edition chapbooks : *The White of the Moon*, (2007) in relation to slavery, *SEAM* (2008) and *Like the Wind Over the Secret* (2009) exploring her rich family history. www.shereemack.com

Hazel Malcolm was born and grew up in the Black Country, West Midlands. She comes from a large Caribbean family which has been a source and inspiration for much of her writing. She enjoys experimenting with various forms of writing, but mainly produces poetry and short stories. She is an active member of several local writing groups and has performed in various locations across the West Midlands.

Jack Mapanje has recently retired as Senior Lecturer in English at Newcastle University. He has published five poetry collections including *Beasts of Nalunga*, which was shortlisted for the Forward Prize for Best Collection (2007). He has edited two African poetry anthologies, *The African Writers' Handbook* and *Gathering Seaweed: African Prison Writing*. He is a recipient of several literary awards.

Valerie Mason-John is the author of six books; she was the winner of the Mind Book of the Year Award for her first novel *Borrowed Body*, which is currently being adapted for a screen play. She was awarded an Honorary Doctorate of Letters by the University of East London for her life-time achievements. www.valeriemason-john.co.uk

Karen McCarthy's pamphlet *The Worshipful Company of Pomegranate Slicers* was selected as a New Statesman Book of the Year in 2006. Her poetry is widely anthologised, most recently in *New Writing 15* (British Council/Granta). She is the editor of the critically acclaimed *Bittersweet: Black Women's Contemporary Poetry* (The Women's Press).

Richard (Rich BLK) Mkoloma is a spoken word MC/poet & fashion designer who works armed with a pen, a voice and a sketchbook. He has performed at numerous venues including Jazz Café, Melweg (Amsterdam), Nuyorican Poets Café and his work has featured on terrestrial and satellite TV. His work as a fashion designer includes Puma, Koshino and Levi's. www.myspace.com/richblk

Raman Mundair is the author of *A Choreographer's Cartography* and *Lovers, Liars, Conjurers and Thieves* (both published by Peepal Tree) and a play, *The Algebra of Freedom.* She is a Rolex Mentor and Protégé Award nominee, a Robert Louis Stevenson Award winner and was identified recently by the BBC/Royal Court Theatre as one of the 'next generation of promising new writers in Britain'. www.ramanmundair.com

Simon M Murray (Sai Mu Rai) is a writer, poet, artist and graphic designer. He teaches creative writing and has performed nationally and internationally. The first part of his novel as memoir, *Kill Myself Now: The True Confessions of an Advertising Genius* is published as a chapbook by Peepal Tree Press. www.myspace.com/saimuraiswords

Daljit Nagra was born and raised in West London and Sheffield. He comes from a Sikh Punjabi background and his poems reflect this experience in content and use of language. His award-winning debut collection is, *Look We Have Coming to Dover!* (Faber & Faber, 2008).

Grace Nichols was born in Guyana and her first collection, *I Is a Long-Memoried Woman*, won the Commonwealth Poetry Prize in 1983. Other collections include *The Fat Black Woman's Poems* and *Sunris*, which won the Guyana Poetry Prize in 1996. Her poems are on the GCSE syllabus and her latest book, *Picasso, I Want My Face Back*, was published by Bloodaxe Books in 2009.

Nqobile Mafu is an actor, singer, artist, playwright and performer. He is the founder and co-director of Vuka Africa Arts, editor of "Ngiyesabanews". He has produced more than ten theatre productions. He a freelance journalist. He self-published a collection of poems, *Ngiyesabain* in 2005. His *Born 2 Speak* was published in 2009.

Tolu Ogunlesi was born in 1982. He is the author of a collection of poetry *listen to the geckos singing from a balcony* (BeWrite Books, 2004). In 2007 he was awarded a Dorothy Sargent Rosenberg poetry prize, and in 2008 the Nordic Africa Institute Guest Writer Fellowship. His poetry has been published in *The London Magazine*, *SABLE Litmag*, *Magma*, and *World Literature Today*.
http://www.felameetsabba.blogspot.com

Nii Ayikwei Parkes is a former International Writing Fellow at the University of Southampton, author of three poetry pamphlets and several short stories and a 2007 recipient of Ghana's National ACRAG award for poetry and literary advocacy. His debut novel *Tail of the Blue Bird* (Jonathan Cape) was published in June 2009. Peepal Tree publishes his poetry collection *The Makings of You* in 2010.
www.niiparkes.com

Janett Plummer is a writer who focuses on the intricate detail of the dust between the cracks. She features in anthologies, *Storm between Fingers, Handmade Fire* and *Flowers on a Shoestring.* Her pamphlet *Lifemarks* is published by flipped eye, mouthmark series. She founded Inspired Word literature charity in 2003. www.theapoets.com

Monika-Akila Richards has written and performed her poetry since 1994. She was a founder member for "Sound Spectrum" theatre group as a playwright and performer. Monika-Akila had her short story "Eleven Years" published by Penguin in an anthology, *True Tales of Mixed Heritage Experience: The Map of Me*. She works in the arts and cultural sector.

Ionie Richards is London-based writer and poet. *A Wolf at My Door* is an autobiographical account of living with lupus. It is her first book, due to be published by Hansib Press. Her work has appeared in *IC3: The Penguin Book of New Black Writing in Britain*, published in 2000.

Roger Robinson was chosen by Decibel as one of 50 writers who have influenced the Black British writing canon over the past 50 years. In 2007 he received a Grants for the Arts Award from the Arts Council. He has published a book of short fiction, *Adventures in 3D* (2001) and a poetry collection, *Suitcase* (2004). His new book, *Suckle*, was published in 2009 by Waterways Press. www.rogerrobinsonbooks.com

Joy Russell is a poet, writer and playwright. Her writing has appeared in numerous publications, including *Crab Orchard*, *Callaloo*, *The Caribbean Writer*, *Velocity: The Best of Apples and Snakes*, *The Fire People: A Collection of Contemporary Black British Poets* and *IC3: The Penguin Book of New Black Writing in Britain*.

Jacob Sam-La Rose's pamphlet, *Communion*, received a Poetry Book Society award in 2006. He is the Artistic Director of the London Teenage Poetry SLAM and an editor for flipped eye press. His poetry has been published in Penguin's *Poems for Love* and *City State: New London Poetry*, among others. www.jsamlarose.com

Denise Saul is a poet, fiction writer and visual artist from London. Her first collection of poetry, *White Narcissi* (flipped eye publishing) was selected Poetry Book Society Pamphlet Choice for Autumn 2007. Her poetry has been published in a variety of UK and US magazines and anthologies.

Sudeep Sen's books include: *Postmarked India: New & Selected Poems*, *Distracted Geographies*, *Rain* and *Aria*. His poetry (translated into 25 languages) and prose features in anthologies by major publishers have been broadcast and appeared in broadsheets including the *TLS*, *The Guardian* and *The Independent*. He was a visiting scholar at Harvard University, and is currently the editorial director of AARK ARTS and editor of *Atlas*. www.atlasaarkarts.net

Seni Seneviratne is a writer, singer, photographer and performer. Her poetry and prose is published in the UK, Denmark, Canada and South Africa. Her debut collection *Wild Cinnamon and Winter Skin* was published in March 2007 by Peepal Tree Press. She is currently working on her second collection.

John Siddique is the author of four collections of poetry; the most recent being *Recital* (SALT). He also writes fiction. He gives readings, mentors and teaches creative writing in the UK and abroad. He was The British Council's Writer in Residence for Los Angeles in summer 2009. www.johnsiddique.co.uk

Sifundo is founder-member of Thea-poets; her current practice focuses on theatre, poetry and site-specific work. Writer-performer for "The Sixth Line" (Hoxton Hall site-specific) "Strictly Come Poetry" and "What Wonder Woman Taught Me". Her poetry features in the anthologies *A Storm Between Fingers* and *Home Is Where The Hatred Is*. www.sifundo.com

Lemn Sissay has published five books of poetry. His latest collection is *Listener* (Canongate). Lemn is an Artist in Residence at the Southbank Centre in Central London. He is patron of The Letterbox Club. In 2009, Lemn received an honorary doctorate from Huddersfield University, and an MBE in 2010. He writes award-winning plays and BBC radio documentaries. http://www.lemnsissay.com

Dorothea Smartt is a poet and live artist. She has published two collections, *Connecting Medium* and *Ship Shape*, both published by Peepal Tree Press. She reads, performs, and exhibits internationally, and regularly goes into schools. She is SABLE LitMag's poetry editor, and Co-Director of Inscribe, a writer development programme based at Peepal Tree Press.

Rommi Smith is a poet and playwright. She has held numerous residencies both nationally and internationally, including most recently, Parliamentary Writer in Residence. This role involved an exploration of the Parliamentary act to abolish the slave trade. This is the first post of its kind in history. Her second collection, *Mornings and Midnights* will be published by Peepal Tree Press. www.rommi-smith.co.uk

Saradha Soobrayen works as a poetry editor for *Chroma* and as a creative arts mentor. Her poems appear in *The Forward Book of Poetry 2008*, *I am twenty people!*, *New Writing 15*, *Oxford Poets Anthology 2007* and *New Poetries IV*. She received an Eric Gregory Award in 2004.

Tina Tamsho-Thomas has enjoyed writing poetry since childhood. Her work is published in several anthologies including: *The Suitcase Book of Love Poems* (Suitcase Press), *Brown Eyes* (Matador), *Sexual Attraction Revealed* (AuthorHouse), *National Poetry Anthology 2006* (United Press). She is currently studying Yoruba and has written her first Yoruba poem.

Marvin Thompson is poet of Jamaican parentage with a special interest in John Coltrane, Walt Whitman and Wales. He also has an MA in Writing from Middlesex University.

Kimberly Trusty is a secondary school teacher based in Birmingham. She holds a Masters degree in Colonial and Post-Colonial Literature from the University of Warwick. Find her on facebook and start up a conversation about the poetry of Derek Walcott, singing cowboys, and/or pirates.

Wangũi wa Goro is a public intellectual, writer, translator, critic, academic and feminist/human rights activist. She has spoken in Europe, USA, Canada and Africa on interdisciplinary interests and received numerous fellowships. Her publications include translations and short stories. Her stories "Heaven and Earth" and "Deep Sea Fishing" have been well-received worldwide.

Gemma Weekes is a poet, singer and all-round scribbler who's debut novel, *Love Me*, has been greeted with rave reviews in *The Guardian* ("a delight"), *The Telegraph* ("hits you where you feel it most") and *The Independent* ("a wonderfully assured debut"). She's performed all over the UK and worked with the likes of Nitin Sawhney and Lyric L. She lives in sunny London with her very cool, very rock 'n' roll boy toddler.

Kaveri Woodward's work has appeared in anthologies and literary journals, including *London Magazine* and *Wasafiri*. Her poetry has been read at Tate Britain, performed by professional actors, and used to develop bharata natyum dance choreography. Kaveri has been awarded several bursaries and prizes. She particularly enjoys cross-arts projects.   http://profile.to/kaveriwoodward